T0193196

I lovingly dedicate this book to *four special Goddesses in my life:* my mom Henny, and my three sisters Cathy, Patricia, and Pamela.

Contents

Section III: Adventuring with the Goddess Within

Acknowledgments

This book could not have been accomplished without the assistance and encouragement of many individuals, to whom I would like to extend my most sincere gratitude.

First and foremost, I am grateful to my husband Bill for his love and support. Throughout my own spiritual journey and several years of writing, he has always encouraged me to do whatever needed to be done to achieve my goals and dreams.

Between my husband, my mom, and my sisters, it is wonderful to have my own team within easy reach whenever I need an enthusiastic boost of support to spur me on – thanks for always serving as my personal cheerleaders!

I extend heartfelt thanks and warm virtual hugs to the many Goddesses (AKA women) who so kindly and willingly shared their personal stories to support this book's *learning through storytelling* approach.

Special thanks to Karen Rowe and Dr. Tony LaMotta who guided and supported me throughout my book-writing journey. Thank you also to Vrinda Pendred for her support in this project.

Finally, kind thanks are extended to Mary, who lovingly shared her talents in creating all the sketches used in this book.

Introduction

"I want to be all that I am capable of becoming."
Katherine Mansfield

I make an attempt to get out of bed, but as my feet touch the floor, my mind switches gears. Instead of standing up, I tuck my legs back under the blankets and lay my head down to escape for a bit longer. It's a weekday. I can smell coffee. Usually, I would be up by now, but I don't feel ready to face the day – after all, what is there to look forward to?

Although not an everyday occurrence, this same scenario has been happening more frequently. I scold myself for being lazy and unmotivated, and try to boost myself up with thoughts of my accomplishments. I like my job and I work hard. I have been married for 30+ years and have raised three amazing sons. I have a beautiful home and the financial means to travel at least once a year. I recently completed back-to-back degrees on either side of 50 and, at the time, I felt happy. But some time has passed and all is not well in my world.

I lie awake and ask myself why I am never satisfied. What's wrong with me? I realize that despite being unhappy with my current situation, I am paralyzed by indecision, inertia, and fear of what and how to change it. Both my internal and external worlds are way out of balance. I am a stuck Goddess!

It strikes me that I am living a disconnect between what my life looks like and what I *want* it to look like. Going deeper, I realize I am suffering from emotional pain, as well. Luckily I have the wherewithal to recognize the need to go on a new journey – not another travel adventure, but a personal journey of self-discovery in order to find and repair both the disconnect and my pain. As a private person who keeps a very tight rein on her emotions and holds her feelings close to her heart, getting to the root cause of these imbalances will take a bit of effort and time – especially in light of my choice to tackle this primarily on my own, rather than working with a counselor.

I know I need help, and as a self-directed learner I immerse myself in exploring a variety of avenues, including visiting several Intuitives and energy healers, attending workshops, and purchasing and reading a vast array of self-help books. Using the tools gathered, I discover that the issues are multiple and complex. I suffer from the "I'm not good enough" syndrome and the often accompanying "I am not lovable" refrain. Another issue lurking in my subconscious mind is the need to face and address how my father's suicide when I was 20 still affects me more than 30 years after the event.

An Intuitive tells me on more than one occasion that I am creating distractions in my life to avoid dealing with my issues. I fill every day to the max, and then wonder why I am unhappy and dissatisfied with all I am seemingly accomplishing. The Intuitive says I don't really know who I am, and even tries to get me to connect with myself. I *so* want this, but it's too soon – I'm just not ready.

* * *

How long can a woman try to be all things to all people and not take anything for herself? How long can she go through life feeling unfulfilled and dissatisfied, not knowing what to do about it, before she recognizes she is truly stuck? How is it possible that a woman can reach the age of 50 and realize she has never really had a relationship with herself and does not know or love the person she is?

What happened to the confident, poised woman who took the world by storm and accomplished everything she set out to accomplish? When and why did that little voice inside her head start to send more negative than positive messages her way? What made her start believing them? When did she stop taking action on her personal goals and dreams? Did she spend so much of her life nurturing others that she forgot to nurture herself? Did she leave unaddressed skeletons in the closet of her mind? How did this woman find herself so restless and stuck, in the prime of her life?

If one or more of these questions resonates with you, you are not alone. Many women feel the same way for a variety of reasons, including a lack of self-awareness, self-love, and self-compassion. Do *you* find yourself surrounded by negativity, or simply so busy doing the countless things you feel you are expected to do (mostly for others), that you forget who you really are and what you want to accomplish in this life?

What was true for our grandmothers and our mothers is true for us – a woman's work is never done! Modern life makes it difficult to be all things to all people and, due to sheer exhaustion, many of us have left our own needs behind. Perhaps we did not realize the importance of nurturing ourselves, or perhaps we were too busy meeting the needs of others. Regardless, we stopped reaching for our goals and dreams, settling for whatever life brought our way, and now we feel something is missing.

In order to live our best life possible, continued personal growth needs to be a top priority. The story opening this introduction is true; it's *my* story. As a lifelong learner and an educator, I spent *years* educating myself in ways that supported my career. Yet, ironically, that very focus was one of the biggest distractions from my necessary personal growth journey. My illuminating moment came during a visit with a dying friend. You will read this story later in this book. An awakening and healing process followed. During this journey, I found many valuable tools to support my personal transformation. Today, I like to say I am a recovering stuck Goddess.

When I recognized several years ago that all was not well in my inner world, I took the necessary action of delving into the root of the problem – my relationship with self. Through my own transformational process, I am grateful to be one of the lucky ones who can happily say I have improved this relationship. As a result, I have identified and am pursuing my life's purpose. My core values, supported by my goals and dreams, along with the powers of the Universe, guide me in bringing that purpose to fruition. My greatest wish is for you to be able to say the same!

25 years ago I re-entered the work world after being a stay-at-home mother for nine years. At that time, I completed a seven-page career planning exercise. The final task was to write a personal mission statement. I wrote, "To have a satisfying relationship with my family, friends, colleagues, and community, and to feel that I am a valuable asset to them all." If I were to rewrite it today, my mission statement would be: "To have a loving relationship with *myself*, my family, friends, colleagues, and extended community, and to support and inspire everyone my life touches to be all that they can be." That includes YOU!

You deserve to spend your days doing what you love, and to feel like you are making a valuable contribution to your own life and the lives of others. Your relationship with yourself is a crucial starting point in achieving these goals. If you are reading this book, I believe it is because you are ready to shake off the life-numbing inertia you have been feeling. You are now ready to embark upon your journey from THIS – stuck and unfulfilled – to BLISS – letting your inner Goddess out to play and living your life with passion!

* * *

Transforming Venus is a comprehensive toolkit designed to support you on this transformational journey. It is filled with my own stories and those of other goddesses of different age groups (30s-70s) from different countries, who have undergone their own unique transformations. It is my wish to help you fast-track your transformation – rather than mirror the weary, meandering route that was my journey.

Transforming Venus is a call for a heightened awareness and fuller experience of the Divine Goddess within. Developing qualities like being loving, compassionate, nurturing, team-focused, intuitive, and caring will help you to embody the wisdom of the Divine Feminine. In ancient Latin, the word *Venus* means "charm." Venus was the Roman Goddess of beauty and love, sex, fertility, and prosperity. Her son was named Cupid. The planet Venus is considered the brightest, most beautiful object in the Universe, next to the sun and the moon. The planet Venus is often referred to as the sister planet to Earth, and Venus boasts flashes of thunder and lightning day and night. So Goddesses, it is our time to live bold and shine brightly, just like the planet Venus!

As the Chinese proverb says:

> *Where there is light in the soul, there will be beauty in the person.*
> *Where there is beauty in the person, there will be harmony in the home.*
> *Where there is harmony in the home, there will be order in the nation.*
> *Where there is order in the nation, there will be peace in the world.*

This is not simply a book to read. It is an educational adventure designed to support you in thinking about and bringing about the necessary life changes you desire and deserve. The book is a combination of head work, heart work, and soul work, divided into three distinct sections. I suggest reading and completing the exercises in the order they appear. Give yourself the gift of *me* time to do this in a quiet, uninterrupted environment.

Section one is designed to awaken the Goddess within and heal the obstacles to her discovery. It will teach you the various ways you can welcome the Divine Feminine wisdom you already possess, which has been lying dormant.

Section two guides you further into transformation and focuses on strategies to nurture and love yourself. You will master techniques to boost your self-confidence and self-esteem, and discover new ways to infuse self-compassion into your life. There is also helpful guidance for increasing your level of positivity and choosing a positive mindset.

Section three focuses on the adventures that await you once you have awakened, healed, nurtured, and embraced your inner Goddess and truly learned to "let her out to play."

I can guarantee positive changes will occur in your life if you apply the techniques, complete the exercises, use the tools provided, and reflect on the stories and information presented. The Goddess in you has a message she wants you to hear. She says her energy has been impatiently waiting to emerge, but you have been blocking it and creating disruption for her. She says, "There are no accidents in life. This book is in your possession because you are ready now; it's your time to grow; it's time to let go and give yourself the gift of letting your inner Goddess out to play!" She sends you her blessing.

Turn the page now and *let the Goddess transformation begin!*

A Note on Reading the Book

Each chapter in this book highlights one of 12 transformational tenets to strive for – something I call the **Goddess Essence Code**. A full list of these tenets is provided below.

1. A Goddess is self-directed. She uses her imagination and courage to invent and envision her own life, which she lives to the fullest on a daily basis.
2. A Goddess is an evolutionary being who recognizes her responsibility to continue to learn and grow, both intellectually and spiritually.
3. A Goddess trusts her intuition and continues to tap into this powerful source of guidance to support her needs.
4. A Goddess possesses imagination, passion, and enthusiasm; and these attributes shine through her very being, supporting her in creating her own destiny.
5. A Goddess is gentle and firm in communicating her boundaries, and protects herself from violation of them.
6. A Goddess understands that everyone experiences pain in life, and she works through her own pain with dignity and courage. She is keenly aware of the need to let go of situations and things that no longer serve her personal growth.
7. A Goddess is committed to peace and harmony, and does her part in healing the earth, as a fundamental principle of her being.

8. A Goddess has a responsibility to respect herself as a sacred being, and to take care of her needs in the physical, sexual, mental, and spiritual sense.
9. A Goddess lives her life authentically, portraying the same façade to the external world as she holds close to her heart.
10. A Goddess has learned balance, and strives to utilize her down time for both personal growth and adventure through play.
11. A Goddess is a generous, joyful being who understands the paramount importance of gratitude and positivity, and expresses these on a daily basis.
12. A Goddess strives to be a cheerleader for the common good of all others who exist in this Universe with her.

Also used are the following **symbols**:

   Indicates Goddess humor moments

   Indicates *A-ha* growth moment opportunities

   Indicates personal development tools

Section I

Awakening and Healing the Goddess Within

Chapter 1

Restless and Stuck

"Nobody's journey is seamless or smooth. We all stumble. We all have setbacks. It's just life's way of saying: time to change course." *Oprah Winfrey*

Goddess Tenet #1: A Goddess is self-directed. She uses her imagination and courage to invent and envision her own life, which she lives to the fullest on a daily basis.

Goddess Jenny, age 57, from Manchester, UK shares her story:

It was the most sweltering summer in years and my body decided this was the perfect time for hot flashes. I was 55 – and entering menopause.

I was terrified. Society had taught me well: in this phase of my life I would be used up, dried up, sagging, nagging, alone, and lonely – a grey lady men wouldn't give a second look and employers would pass up for someone glowing with youth and promise.

I floundered.

At the same time, my two boys, both in their 20s, decided it was time to leave home (although I begged them not to). I walked out of yet another low-paying, mind-numbing job with a boss who held me squashed under his thumb and groped me every time he walked by. I dated a string of unavailable men, pretending to be single but hiding their long-time loves from me. Canvasses and notebooks begging me to paint and write remained blank and empty.

Suddenly I was no longer a mother, no longer an employee, no longer a lover, no longer creative. It was as if I was no longer a woman.

I crashed.

It was a big crash, a "no light at the end of the tunnel" crash. An "I have nothing more to offer" crash. An "I really am alone" crash. An "I am going to wither up and die" crash.

I knew I had to do something, but I didn't know what. The days went by, and I felt like that old grey lady, stuck and restless. Not that I didn't have any creative ideas; I just couldn't muster up the mental energy to do anything about them.

I read a lot, watched movie after movie, but that only made me feel like a voyeur, an outsider looking in on someone else's fabulous life. I was a watcher instead of a doer, a blurry background character in the story of my life. With the little energy I had, and an on-again, off-again shrouded flicker of ... hope? ... urging me forward, I found myself at the unemployment office, where I was offered a back-to-school grant. As long as I took something that rendered me employable (i.e. not art, not writing), I had a chance to go back to school. They suggested Esthetics. I thought, "Makeover!" and agreed.

The first day of class in January, I walked into a room of 20-odd gorgeous, bright, amazing girls – all in their 20s – who looked up at me and smiled in unison.

"Nope, not the teacher!" I grinned, embarrassed, and slinked away to an empty chair at the back of the class.

I quickly became the resident "mom" and those girls, my little ducklings, rejuvenated me, entertained me, astounded me, and challenged me.

By the end of December I graduated with honors, maintaining an A+ average the entire year (I had to prove something to those young'uns, after all!). Unfortunately, after working at three different spas, I came to realize it was nothing to do with client care and everything to do with selling $200 face creams that absolutely did not work. My honesty won out and I quit the business.

But I'd had a taste of this new outside world of opportunities and I liked it.

Next, I was accepted into a community Self-Employment Program, which funded me for a year while I took business classes and facilitated the start-up of my home business as an artist. Yep, art! I am now a professional commissioned artist, writing books on the side, in a spacious studio in my own home. Just last week I finished the basement, and it is now set up for Relaxation Massage/Reiki/Reflexology sessions.

So, little by little, I burst out of the myths of menopause dictated to me by society.

Everything was a positive change. I was no longer a slave to my body; in fact, I gained a sexual control over it I never thought possible. As my estrogen diminished, the emotional roller coaster turned into a pleasant ferris wheel ride. The clarity of mind! The opening of the heart! The shifting of the soul! The blossoming of the spirit!

Not to mention, I created my own work schedule so I can take my Yorkies on extra long walks during the day, dance Zumba twice a week, and enjoy coffee breaks with my sis. I guess all along it was freedom I was searching for, a non-conforming lifestyle, where I could finally be ... myself.

The best part was I found a home in the embrace of the loving arms of my sisters, who had endured this rite of passage before me – a welcome home. The competition of our younger, immature selves was gone, leaving only camaraderie and communal energy. I am enjoying an empowerment I never dreamed existed, a coming of age with a lifetime of lessons learned, problems solved, and experiences both good and bad, with massive doses of humility, empathy, and gratitude.

3

Our Goddess Journey

From entering menstruation in our early teens, to approaching or having already experienced menopause as mature Goddesses, we have been on a constant adventure of growing and learning. Between these two experiences is a long period (pun intended) of building our lives, our relationships, our families, and our careers. How many of us use that time to nourish and build *ourselves?* We arrive at the current point feeling stuck, restless, and often alone.

Innumerable things can shake our confidence and happiness, notwithstanding the female hormonal fluctuations that make up our Goddess nature. Every one of us has our own story; no two women have lived the same journey. And there are just as many life events that may be major contributing factors to Goddess *stuckness* as there are stuck Goddesses. Yet as we approach the middle portion of our life, it is important to recognize that the real gift inherent in this phase is the invitation to change. Indeed, menopause is commonly referred to as "the change." This time is ripe for us to begin to do what we need to do to free ourselves.

But what's been keeping us stuck in the first place? How do so many of us find ourselves moving into our golden years so out of sync with our higher selves?

Sometimes, relationships keep us stuck. We constantly aspire to new goals and dreams as we age, and sometimes our partners don't keep up. We long to fly free, while our partners can't wait to put their feet up after a long working life. We may have continued to learn and grow at a rate our partner didn't. All these things may contribute to the feeling of being stuck in a relationship that no longer meets our needs.

Sometimes, it is the dependence created by relationships that are decades long that keeps us stuck. We might feel deeply unhappy, yet dependent. The work it takes to disentangle ourselves from our partners emotionally, financially, and physically feels so overwhelming that instead we choose to stay stuck.

Then there is the *stuckness* that might come from already being out of a relationship and paralyzed by fear of the unknown – or not being in a relationship at all and feeling the fear of being alone – or a fear of having too many choices, or a lack of knowledge about how to move forward. Sometimes we're just afraid to take the wrong step. In those instances, often we make no decision at all, and stay stuck in the dismal, helpless, lonely, and paralyzing status quo.

Even beyond the significant physical shift we experience as midlife approaches, life is full of shifts and changes. For those of us who were able to stay at home to raise our children, suddenly we're faced with an empty nest. If we have not worked, we might see returning to the workforce as an extremely daunting task. We've been CEO of the home and VP of child-rearing, yet we're intimidated when it comes to finding a new job. We lack confidence, fear our skills are not up to par, and worry no one will want our services.

If we were working all along, our jobs, just like our relationships, may have stagnated. The energy of change is all around us. We feel less and less satisfied by what we once delighted in, or we are not learning, growing, or challenging ourselves in the same way. We recognize that we are growing older, time is short, and we want to fulfill our desires to be challenged and satisfied.

Whatever reason we feel stuck, the very action of our physical bodies changing in such a profound way is a strong impetus for us to create the changes we seek in our lives. Our bodies, in their wisdom, are incredibly helpful in motivating us to make the changes we require to live out our lives in the most vibrant and vital way possible, and re-establish a connection with our authentic self.

When Is It My Turn to Be Nurtured?

Regardless of what is keeping you stuck right now, chances are you have been nurturing and giving to others in a significant way throughout your life. It's natural; to be feminine is to give. While living our busy, full lives, we have spent a large portion of time focusing on the needs of others and not nearly enough on our own needs, including (of critical importance!) our continuing personal development. Yet how can we celebrate our true Goddess selves if we do not nurture our very essence?

The mistake many of us make is expecting to be nurtured externally. We believe we have given of ourselves so much that someone ought to give back to us. But the truth is *we need to learn to nurture ourselves*. Real nurturing, that is lasting and empowering, is that which we give to ourselves.

This is the journey we must undertake, wherein we critically assess our identities, attitudes, values, and beliefs. This is our opportunity to reflect on what we think and believe, and how we act. As we continue to learn and grow, we access new knowledge and skills not available to us when we were younger. Many of us have been raised to believe "it's not all about you," but I am telling you now, *it **is** all about you!* This is an inside job. Moving to the better place of living our authentic life, the life we are meant to live as mature Goddesses, is entirely up to us.

There is a saying that resonates with me: "God made us age so we realize we cannot afford to waste any time in our lives." To me this translates as, "Goddesses, let's get going!"

Change

> "The changes we dread most may contain our salvation." *Barbara Kingsolver*

Change means uncertainty about the future, and that makes many of us uncomfortable. For example, frogs are not very "change-adept." If you put a frog in a pot of water and put the pot on a burner set to high, the frog will not hop out. Instead, it will stay in the water, despite the rising temperature – and we all know how that story ends. As women of wisdom who have had many experiences in life, we have a great degree of capacity for change (much more so than a frog). We know better than to stay in a pot on its way to boil – yet many of us do … *and find ourselves in hot water!*

We must acknowledge that our greatest barrier to change is ourselves! As change is the only constant in life, we need to learn to be *adaptable*. The Goddess will strive to become a woman who welcomes change, adapts to change – and thrives. Thriving through change may feel like a lofty goal. Start by becoming a change agent in your own life, by growing your awareness and recognizing that *you are the change you wish to see!* How do you get there? Start by honestly assessing yourself and your current life situation. You do this through the lens of self-reflection and an examination of your thoughts, beliefs, behaviors, and feelings. But we'll get to that.

The Phases of Change

Change takes place when we replace old, comfortable, and familiar processes, environments, and social networks with new and unfamiliar ones. This may challenge your comfort and confidence levels. You are replacing something you are accustomed to with something unknown or very different.

Abandoning the old and familiar is often associated with an emotional upheaval, much like the grieving process. When we are faced with experiences like the end of a long-term relationship, or a major career change, or any significant event that results in a loss in our lives, it is actually a form of grieving. There is a *letting go* that needs to occur, a series of emotions that need to be felt, and we can either hang on tight and resist the sweeping current of change, or release and evolve into the Goddess we are becoming. We can see this change as a problem, or perceive it as the opportunity it truly is.

In order for true transformational change to occur, we need to go through various transitional phases. Each phase moves us closer to the next and, ultimately, toward complete transformation. Different coping strategies may be needed at various stages of this process for us to succeed and move forward.

The first phase includes feelings of disbelief and shock: "Why is this happening to me?" We are blindsided by a sizeable shift interrupting our life as we know it, whatever it may be.

Phase two includes depression or re-hashing the situation over and over in our mind. In this phase, we might realize we can't go back to the way things were, but we have yet to determine what the change means to us, and we don't know how to move forward. How will we fit into the new life we are supposed to create? Can we even do this? These and other life changes can be major setbacks for many of us, and there will be a period of adjustment while we process.

As time passes, our goal becomes to transition into the acceptance phase, where we recognize the need to move forward and have developed a deeper understanding of where we might fit into the new picture, as well as how we can make some positive adjustments. We may even be able to plan and implement some necessary steps to move us closer to our newly developed goals.

Reaching the acceptance phase may well be where many get stuck. If you can't get past the depression and re-hashing phase, you may need guidance to move through it. This book is designed to help you in this.

 As a new grandma, I am beginning to believe no one likes change except a wet baby.

Feelings of discomfort toward change are both natural and expected. It's nice to know we are not alone, and that our emotional reactions and discomfort are considered normal – but how do we address this uncertainty?

Our desire to change can be sparked by either positive or negative motivators. A positive motivator may be our keen desire to live our life's purpose. This kind of change is powerful because it represents an internal driving force pushing us to develop and grow as we strive to attain our goals. Jenny's *return to school* story at the start of this chapter is an example of this.

A negative motivator may be the dismal state of affairs our life has become; we know change is the only solution to our survival. Sometimes a negative experience forces change upon us and leads us to take a new series of action steps.

Transformational change is not a one-time event. In order to remake ourselves, we have to undergo constant self-reflection – which includes homework! And as your Goddess coach, I am assigning your first piece of transformational learning.

The good: I am going to guide you through the process.

The bad: I can only be your guide; the real work is your own.

The ugly: You have to examine your behavior and emotions honestly and without judgment.

 ## Exercise: Visualization

Close your eyes for a moment and envision your ideal life. Dream large! Consider the ultimate goal to be "living boldly and shining brightly." And use your imagination. If nothing comes through clearly, make something up.

You might dream of changing careers, going back to school, focusing on past or newly adjusted goals, downsizing your home, moving to another place, moving on from a relationship that is no longer serving you, starting out fresh with new goals – or something else entirely.

See yourself in harmony with yourself and others, moving forward with a defined purpose and living your passion. Picture some exciting changes to your life; see yourself having fun and being happy.

Be open to new possibilities. Remember: you are the star on this stage of life; others merely play supporting roles. Don't let them steal your thunder!

Now I challenge you to focus on what is really important to you, as you move forward into living the life you have visualized and dreamed about.

 Look in the mirror and see the one person who can change your situation – and the only one you control.

Exercise: Identifying the Problem(s) through Self-Reflection

"Much of the time we are transfixed by all the ways we can reflect ourselves into the world and barely find the time to reflect back deeply into our own selves."
Ariel Garten

It is easy to know we are stuck, and less easy to discern *why*. We may know part of the reason, but not have identified the magnitude of the whole situation, or the impact of the choices we have made and continue to make. We need to understand this before we can become unstuck. Although this may sound simple, many of us do not consider it important. We don't reflect and analyze the situation fully, and therefore never get to the root of the problem. This is a critical first step to developing strategies to reverse the situation.

For this next exercise, I am inviting you to – you guessed it – reflect on choices you have made in your life that may have contributed to you feeling stuck. We are our greatest barriers to change. Don't hold yourself back from the potential life has to offer you.

Place a tick in the appropriate boxes below, noting the choices you have made.

Marriage

To marry (have remained happily married)	☐
Not to marry (have remained happily single)	☐
To marry (things did not work out, nasty divorce)	☐
To marry (things did not work out, divorce went OK)	☐
To marry (things did not work out, currently separated)	☐
To marry (things did not work out, but a subsequent marriage did)	☐
To marry (but never found the right life partner)	☐
To marry (but sadly, life partner died)	☐

Children

To have children (aptly blessed with them)	☐
Not to have children	☐
To have children (sadly not gifted with them)	☐
Not to have children (blessed with them anyway)	☐
To have children (sadly one of them taken through divorce)	☐
To have children (sadly lost one of them through death)	☐

Education

High school education (attended as planned)	☐
High school education (life got in the way and this did not happen)	☐
College education (attended as planned)	☐
Did not attend college	☐
College education (life intervened, did not get to complete)	☐

Job/Career

A job/career (happily lived this choice)	☐
A job/career (but life intervened, e.g. relocation, downsizing, job loss, etc.)	☐
To be a stay at home mom (was able to live this goal)	☐
To be a stay at home mom (but a life situation forced me back to work)	☐
To work part-time and be with my children when not working	☐
Happily retired	☐
Unhappily retired (bored)	☐

Health/Wellness

I have remained relatively healthy with no major health challenges	☐
A personal injury/illness/disease majorly impacts my life	☐
A loved one's injury/illness/disease majorly impacts my life	☐

A recent change in my financial status is majorly impacting my life ☐

The death of a close friend is majorly impacting my life ☐

Recent changes to my eating/sleeping habits are majorly impacting my life ☐

Additional Items

_____ ☐

_____ ☐

_____ ☐

_____ ☐

_____ ☐

Now take some time to reflect on your list of ticked items. Do you see any patterns, tendencies, or other notable *a-ha* moments? What stands out as the most relevant point you have recognized here?

_____

_____

_____

_____

Has this reflection allowed you to see why some of your decisions may have caused you to be stuck?

_____

_____

_____

_____

Now, take a few moments to document what you have learned about yourself from this reflection, and consider how you can apply this new learning in the future.

_____

_____

_____

_____

Chapter 2

The Problem with Being Restless and Stuck

"No beating yourself up. That's not allowed. Be patient with yourself. It took you years to form the bad habits of thought that you no longer want. It will take a little time to form new and better ones. But I promise you this: even a slight move in this direction will bring you some peace. The more effort you apply to it, the faster you'll find your bliss, but you'll experience rewards immediately." *Holly Mosier*

Goddess Tenet #6: A Goddess understands that everyone experiences pain in life, and she works through her pain with dignity and courage. She is keenly aware of the need to let go of situations and things that no longer serve her personal growth.

Goddess Dani, age 48, from Breda, The Netherlands tells her story:

My stepfather was a violent man with a "taste" for little girls, and I was the closest little girl available. I suffered at his hand for many years. When I was 12 years old, I told on him. I wanted my mother to save me like she said she would, but she was unable to leave him and I was sent away to a foster home. I made a decision never to trust another human being again. I also decided I wasn't worthy of protection or love.

I met my first boyfriend a few years later – another man who would abuse me. Perhaps I chose him because deep inside, that is what I felt I deserved.

Three months after my 18ᵗʰ birthday, I decided the abuse was just too great and broke up with him. Late that night, he came back to my home. My door flew open and he walked in with the eyes of a crazed man, angry, yelling. When he saw me, we locked eyes. He pulled a gun out of his pocket and said, "I love you, Dani. I hope you're happy! Here – watch this!" He put the gun to his head and pulled the trigger. I watched his eyes as he died. I can't even begin to tell you what it does to your soul to witness something like that. To wonder why I was still alive. To feel guilty for taking care of myself. To be afraid to take care of myself ever again. I made an even deeper decision never to trust another human again. I followed that up with the decision that human connections, love, vulnerability, and happiness were unsafe for me. I also knew I was never going to be safe.

The stress I felt was unbearable. Emotionally and physiologically, I was a mess. For the next eight years, I drank myself to sleep. I was afraid of everyone and everything around me. I was unable to make any real connections with anyone. All my relationships were built on fear – too afraid to be alone, yet too afraid to let myself connect with people, and terrified to break up with anyone. I demolished relationships instead of ending them. I became skilled at putting on "the face" of someone who was OK. I didn't want to talk to anyone about myself or my feelings. I didn't want anyone to try to help me. I just wanted to be invisible.

I got sober at the age of 26. I found an outlet as a musician, and became a spiritual teacher and public speaker. I found the pain I had endured could help people, and I poured honesty into every word I let out. I helped thousands of people over the years. I became good at appearing confident, outgoing, happy, and full of hope and wisdom. I had a talent for helping people heal their scars. But if anyone tried to get too close to me, I would pull away. I kept myself busy helping others. I didn't need friends; I just needed to be there for everyone but myself. I kept myself safe from deep connections. I was the one person everyone came to when they had problems in their relationships. I helped others do what I wouldn't do myself, which was get close to others. Then along came Tiffany.

Tiffany was a 14-year-old cancer patient addicted to pain pills. I ended up being her mentor. Over the next few years, we developed a very close relationship. I knew what it was like to feel alone and like someone upstairs had it out for me. Tiffany had had cancer since she was seven years old. I loved Tiffany with every inch of my being. I was also terrified of her since she was sick and, therefore, could possibly leave me sometime. But she needed me, and I felt I was meant to help her. She confided in me things she said she could never tell another human being. No matter how much I wanted to run, I could never stay gone. Eventually, she and her family would name me her Godmother. It was truly an honor I felt I didn't deserve.

She had complications and was in and out of the hospital frequently. One time, I showed up and it looked like it was the end. I was terrified. When she came to, she had her parents ask me to come see her, but I was afraid, so I found reasons why I couldn't show up. I'm not proud of that. I told her that later. She understood, but told me she needed me – even if I was afraid.

At the age of 24, Tiffany finally found a donor and had a bone marrow transplant. Exactly one year to the day of her transplant, the cancer returned. She had a seizure and ended up in the hospital. She went blind. The doctors said she had two weeks to two months left to live.

As I sat on the bed with her alone one night, I said to her, "So, you're blind now." She laughed and said, "Yep." So I asked, "If everything in this world happens for a reason, why do you think you're blind?" She sat for minutes before she said, "You know, Mama –" (a term her *family had asked if she could call me)* "– I used to think it mattered what my makeup looked like, how my hair looked, how much fat I had on my stomach. But it took me going blind to see anything at all. The only thing that matters is LOVE. People can give me a trip, or money, or a new car … none of those things matter to me. I'm blind, I'm going to die, and all I want anyone to bring me is LOVE."

Those words hit me like a ton of bricks. My whole life changed. I realized that in the end, all the people I had helped would probably come to say thank you to me. I had helped so many others heal their relationships, but I hadn't done that for myself.

Tiffany died a few months later. I slept with her in her bed. I talked to her almost every day. I wrote notes for her to everyone she loved. I handed out those notes after she passed away. I had become intimate with another human being I knew would leave me. I was afraid, but she had cleared it all up for me. It didn't matter how many people I helped to heal. I needed to help myself heal as well. I realized loss is a part of life. But even scarier than being afraid of losing a person to death is losing out on the connection we could have while they are here – in front of us.

Since she passed, I have connected to every human being I've ever wanted to – including my sweet mother, who I now see didn't abandon me, but was actually trying to protect me the best way she knew how, which was to get me out of the situation she was in and make sure I was safe.

Tiffany not only changed my life; she changed the lives of everyone around me, as well. She healed my heart by breaking it. All that time, I thought I was here to help save her. But she was here to save me. She made me whole. I am now the woman I used to pretend to be. I achieved this by being willing to be vulnerable, even if it hurt – even if I am afraid. Bringing love to everything I do is the way of empowerment now. I walk through my fears. I "live" again … and I embrace every moment I have left.

So perhaps, in retrospect, I am not the Goddess in this story; Tiffany is.

* * *

Some of us, like Dani, have kept ourselves stuck because of beliefs we took on to protect ourselves from pain. For others, being stuck may have crept up on us while we weren't paying attention, waking up wondering where our lives have gone.

It doesn't matter how that looks for you; we are all in this together. Are we not all striving for fulfillment? It is my hope that you might see where your current *stuckness*, for whatever reason, is hindering your ability to grow and develop.

 And I mean intellectually, spiritually, and from a positive personal growth and development perspective.

 I am not referring to any physical growth! We Goddesses are done with that phase of our growth and development!

We all have a unique journey to experience, and the more positive and compassionate with ourselves we can be when making choices on this journey, the fewer regrets we will have when we are older and wiser. This journey is much more challenging when you are focused on your problems because that does not allow your mind to be open to the solution. Sometimes we get stuck in the past with things and people that have wronged us, and the related issues repeat through our heads like a broken record. If this dysfunctional record is playing a negative verse, we'll just reinforce the negative thought patterns.

Thank Goodness for Goddess Progress

> "Progress is the product of human agency. Things get better because we make them better. Things go wrong when we get too comfortable, when we fail to take risks or seize opportunities." *Susan Rice*

If you were a Goddess 50 years ago, chances are pretty good you would not have even been looking for this book because your life was the way it was and there was nothing you could do about it. And if you *were* purchasing a book for yourself, your husband likely gave you the money to buy it, likely influenced your voting preference, and it may well have been *him* rather than *you* who was asked to sign the consent form for any procedure *you* were to undergo, including delivering *your* baby from *your* body. In many families, including my own, financial provision was only made for the male child to attend college. Women mostly worked in the home, and any who were working outside the home were let go from their jobs once their pregnancy became visible.

We have come a long way since then, and while we may not all be the top earners in the household, we now *control* and manage more wealth than ever. In their article *Women Control the Purse Strings*, Nielson, experts in studying consumers, report that the Fleishman-Hillard Inc. brand marketing experts have estimated women will control two-thirds of the consumer wealth in the United States over the next ten years. This will make women the beneficiaries of the largest wealth transference in the country's history.[1]

 Yes, in many cases we women are the ones handing out the pocket money, now!

As we have gained more freedom, more autonomy, more education and more economic power, you would think we would have gained more happiness and contentment, but that is not necessarily the case. A 2009 study by researchers Betsey Stevenson and Justin Wolfers, entitled *The Paradox of Declining Female Happiness*,[2] has shown that measures of women's subjective wellbeing has fallen to below those of men. The happiness trend has shifted toward men and away from women, the opposite of what was reported in the 1970s. It seems we are not alone; there are a lot of stuck, stressed Goddesses out there! What gives?

---

[1] http://www.nielsen.com/us/en/insights/news/2013/u-s--women-control-the-purse-strings.html

[2] http://www.nber.org/papers/w14969.pdf

The rise of our advancement in the workforce has not been matched with a similar rise in the sharing of duties in the family. That is, while women are welcome in the workforce, we have yet to see a full embracing of stay-at-home dads, or men subscribing to a more equal approach to housework. This has left many Goddesses with full-time careers *and* households to manage. We have many duties, people to please, and so many demands on our time.

To top it all off, life today is far more complex than ever before. On a daily basis, the various media sources exploit the injustice, violence, and suffering that occurs in the world. Add numerous frustrations, conflicts, and problems that continually develop and it would be surprising to find any woman out there not experiencing some level of stress.

 Wouldn't it be a breath of fresh air to have a positivity news channel where all the good things that occur in people's lives were shared with others!

The good news is having some knowledge of the role stress plays, and some techniques in your back pocket to minimize it, will help reduce long-term bad stress.

Stress

> "Before you agree to do anything that might add even the smallest amount of stress to your life, ask yourself: *What is my truest intention?* Give yourself time to let a *yes* resound within you. When it's right, I guarantee your entire body will feel it." *Oprah Winfrey*

According to Merriam Webster, stress is "a state of mental tension and worry caused by problems in your life, work."[3] Researchers generally agree that a certain amount of stress is inevitable and

---

[3] http://www.merriam-webster.com/dictionary/stress

normal. What the dictionary *doesn't* tell you is there are two kinds of stress: good stress (*eustress*) and bad stress (*distress*). Bad stress over a long period of time can become ugly – but good stress can actually be helpful!

Eustress

> "My body needs laughter as much as it needs tears.
> Both are cleansers of stress." *Mahogany Silver Rain*

 I would like to introduce you to your new best friend: eustress!

In order to experience joy, you must feel stress. Joy is good, and the good stress that goes hand in hand with it is known as eustress.

Consider a job interview with a positive outcome, where you responded well to all the questions but were surprised because you were so nervous. That was your eustress at work, pumping you up with motivation to get the job done and get it done well.

Have you ever watched in anticipation and excitement one of your children or grandchildren compete in a competition?

Remember your first date? If you are married, remember walking down the aisle at your wedding?

If you have children, you also more than likely felt joy and happiness during their delivery.

 You can't tell me that wasn't stressful!

 You were nervous and excited in all these examples of eustress!

Eustress helps with your concentration and focus. It plays a major role in your motivation and allows you to rise above your challenges. On a physical front, you feel good stress when you work out. If you have ever participated in a kickboxing or Zumba class, or even gone for an exhilarating bike ride, you know your body was stressed in new and challenging ways and it felt good.

 Well, maybe not so much the next day!

This same type of positive stress can occur in the emotional, spiritual, and intellectual areas of your life, too. Without being pushed past your Goddess limits, and without being encouraged to live boldly and shine brightly, you wouldn't grow. If eustress is the positive fuel for our accomplishments and successes, then Goddesses, get ready for some positive changes!

While undergoing good stress, your system releases chemicals into your bloodstream. This happens during bad stress too, but the chemical compositions are different; during eustress, feel-good chemicals are released. Your life will be greatly improved if you can maximize the eustress in your life. Throughout this book, there will be a focus on how to add more eustress to your life.

Moving from Distress to De-stress!

"Give your stress wings and let it fly away."
Terri Guillemets

How we feel stress is highly subjective. One woman can feel stressed about something that another would consider insignificant or may even feel energized by.

 You know those Wonder Woman types? Nothing ever seems to faze them!

Stress is not just a feeling, though; it's an actual physiological response to a threat. When you encounter a perceived threat – if someone yells at you, for instance – a part of your brain sets off a reactive alarm system in your body. Through a combination of signals, your body responds to this stress in a number of ways. Your blood vessels constrict; your breathing, pulse, and blood pressure increase and more stress hormones flow through your bloodstream. One such hormone, adrenaline, causes your heart rate and blood pressure to rise, and boosts your energy. This is why in times of great stress people accomplish heroic and unheard of challenges, such as lifting a car off a person.

In the short term, these hormones support us in getting through the required situation; but once the situation is over, they are designed to shut off. If the stressors continue and the hormones continue to be produced, our body system is disrupted with the long-term activation of the stress-response system. Significant health problems can result from chronic stress due to overexposure to stress hormones, so it is important that stress be dealt with and kept at a healthy level.

According to The Free Dictionary by Farlex, it is now believed that 80-90% of all disease is stress-related.[4] The signs of stress can manifest in our bodies in several different ways, including cognitive, emotional, and physical. These manifestations can start out as minor inconveniences, but if they are not addressed, they can escalate and cause debilitating health concerns.

The American Institute of Stress states that both their clinical and experimental research supports the fact that when we are living with a sense of having little or no control over a situation, we will find this distressful.[5]

 Are you seeing a connection here with feeling restless and stuck?

We need some stress-coping techniques to support us through our transformation. The mastery and long-term practice of these techniques will help us remain calmer and more effective in high-pressure situations. Their continued use will also help us avoid the

---

[4]   http://medical-dictionary.thefreedictionary.com/Stress
[5]   http://www.stress.org/education

potential of prolonged stress and the imminent health deterioration that goes with it. We need to get from distress to de-stress!

 ## Stress Management Exercises and Tools

There are all kinds of ways to manage stress. Here are just a few of the more traditional stress management techniques. Remember, relaxation is key.

Stress Relief / Deep Breathing

This is one of the most popular ways to calm down quickly when you are stressed. You may want to use this technique when entering a meeting that is critical to your future (job interview, important work-related meeting, promotion meeting, etc.). It can be done by anyone, the results are immediate, no special training is required, and it costs nothing.

Take a deep breath and feel your abdomen expand. Breathe in through your nose, hold the breath for a few seconds, and then exhale through your mouth. Take twice as long to exhale as you took to inhale. Complete 4-8 of these breath cycles 1-3 times a day, or prior to the meeting or other stressful event you are facing.[6]

Laughter

Research has repeatedly shown that the benefits of laughter are far-reaching. When you have a good belly laugh, several things occur. Your mental load is lightened, and some physical changes take place in

---

[6] http://www.marksdailyapple.com/deep-breathing/#axzz41bNN3kh4

your body that support stress relief. Laughter is definitely something we need to add more of to our lives. Here are some suggestions for how to add more laughter to your life:

- Switch your focus to comedies, when you watch movies or TV shows.
- Plan to spend more time with friends who make you laugh.
- Look for the humor in life's daily trials and tribulations; take the emphasis off the frustration and find a chuckle in the situation, instead.
- Have more fun doing what you like with friends.
- Don't leave laughter to chance; take a proactive approach to bringing more laughter into your day-to-day life. You will be glad you did!

Laughter Yoga

Laughter and yoga both have so many stress-busting benefits; why not combine them? Laughter yoga is a playful, infectious way to feel a whole lot better, both mentally and physically. One research study into the effects of laughter yoga on the stress levels of participants found that positive emotions increased by 17% and negative emotions dropped by 27%. Additionally, perceived stress dropped considerably.[7] WOW! Sign me up!

Find a club near you at http://www.laughteryoga.org. This global movement for better health, more joy, and world peace is growing rapidly, with over 6,000 clubs worldwide. On the site you enter your country, province/state, and city and find the nearest laughter club to you. It's that simple.

---

[7]   http://www.laughteryoga.org/english/laughteryoga/details/315

Music

Research studies[8] have shown that Baroque music has a very relaxing effect on the body. This genre of music has also been found to improve memory and our capacity to learn. To get you started, I recommend the 42-minute Vivaldi piece entitled *The Four Seasons*, which can easily be found online for free.

* * *

We aren't helping ourselves by putting others first or running ourselves ragged trying to please everyone. Stress is no laughing matter; and before we can even begin to do the personal growth work required, we must recognize where we are stressed, and vow to apply some kind of relaxation and stress management practice to our lives.

Part of awakening and healing the Goddess within is learning to love ourselves fully and with fierce commitment. No matter what your path to healing looks like, the judgment stops here, the stress lessens now, and the journey continues.

---

[8] http://education.jhu.edu/PD/newhorizons/strategies/topics/Arts%20in%20 Education/brewer.htm

Chapter 3

Exploring Your Spirituality

"[Wo]man is in reality a spiritual being and only when [s]he lives in the spirit is [s]he truly happy."
Abdu'l-Baha [author modifications to feminine]

Goddess Tenet #2: A Goddess is an evolutionary being who recognizes her responsibility to continue to learn and grow, both intellectually and spiritually.

Goddess Eliza, age 36, from New York, United States tells her story:

"Spirituality doesn't need religion; religion needs spirituality."

I first heard those words from Mike Dooley, one of the featured teachers from "The Secret", also known for his free "Notes from the Universe."[9] It was not the first time I'd considered both the connection

---

[9]   www.tut.com/about/mikedooley

and the difference between spirituality and religion. Nonetheless, those words were the truth-bomb I needed and the final liberation on my spiritual path. As I became assured in my own unique spiritual practices, it became something of a mantra in the months that followed.

Spiritual identity and practice were concepts I was raised to accept as a part of life, in the same way I learned to tie my shoes and brush my teeth. There are no childhood memories without some tie to my conservative Christian upbringing: Sunday school and songs about Jesus, Bible verses at home with my parents, volunteering and babysitting through the church. I even calculate my age by memories of overseas mission trips.

To my way of thinking, this provided me with a wonderful advantage. I grew up with the knowledge of unconditional love. I knew there was so much more than the physical plane of existence, that I had a soul, and that my soul would live forever. I saw both strong and weak examples of faith and had a sense of what I wanted to emulate.

Advantages aside, I came to the end of my sheltered time at home with serious misgivings, doubts, and emptiness. There was too much that didn't add up, too much I couldn't qualify. As I became exposed to the world outside my bubble, I realized I was a minority. I chafed against the notion that all these wonderful people I met who didn't believe as I did were condemned to eternal damnation. I chafed against the belief that my gay friends in theater and music were sinners. I floundered for months before I awakened to the reality that this entire identity was not mine at all, though I had played my part admirably. There was no way forward and something had to give.

I decided to let it all go, bit by bit. I studied and asked questions. For the first time in my life, I could hear my inner voice and I began to listen. I felt relief and elation, but the initial excitement of this adventure wore off quickly as news of my choice reached those at home. Former friends left in droves, some even warned by their parents to avoid me. Sadness overtook my joy as I realized that the only community and identity I had ever known had no space for me. None of those friends had ever been real friends, only relationships of convenience based on proximity. I was on my own in every sense, and devastation grew into inner rage.

Years of anger followed, directed at the God I thought I knew and his Christian followers. I focused on bad examples of faith – and there were plenty to choose from. I had all the evidence I needed to hang the "CLOSED" sign on my heart and sink into bitterness. I found myself in abusive relationships, self-mutilating and starving myself. I had been betrayed and kicked to the curb to figure myself out alone, and those feelings had nowhere to go, so they manifested in my body and on my flesh. In the darkest times, I didn't care if I lived or died.

Thankfully, the glimmer of light within and the greater plan for my life were not snuffed out. One day, I found myself in a yoga class. For the first time, I focused on the good things my body could do and my mind was quiet for a brief time. I grabbed onto yoga like a life preserver and hung on for dear life. I'll never forget the first time I heard my instructor deliver a message of unconditional self-acceptance and love. It was directed toward the body and yoga practice, but it stirred something deep inside me that I thought I had destroyed.

I went home that day and cried. I asked if I might not be lost and alone, after all. The instant response was that I was never alone and never would be. I decided to set my worldview on fire for the second time, only this time I begged to be happy. I was still angry. I still felt broken and beyond repair, but I entertained the notion that perhaps one day I might not be. I held everything I knew with open hands and let it go, so long as I might just be happy.

I built my new spiritual practice around yoga and gratitude, and have watched myself grow and blossom in ways I never could have dreamed. I now know that every bit of the dark period was divinely directed for my greatest glory. As the author of my life, I get to choose the story's perspective. I have chosen to reclaim everything that has ever happened to me as purpose-driven, even sacred. I have forgiven my abusers, including myself. God has many names to me now and I see Source energy everywhere.

By the time I found myself listening to Mike Dooley, I had come a long, long way. Still, his words washed over me and I saw that *the adventure was only beginning. Since that day, more than three years ago, my spiritual expansion and practice has accelerated at an unimaginable pace. I have answered my calling to share my stories and teach. What I now tell others is that spirituality doesn't need religion, but it does need YOU. You are the most important part of the equation! Your spiritual practice and beliefs create an imprint entirely unique to you. The world needs more authentic, connected women. Welcome your spiritual identity with open arms, explore, and see what adventures wait for you.*

Our Soul Signature

Our intentions allow us to recognize the paramount relationship between our self and our environment. It is intention that sets positive energy in motion, and we can use this power to tackle any challenge we want to overcome.

Throughout this book, the focus is on spirituality in a non-religious context. You are free to use your own personal religious affiliation to complement your experience. This is your journey and I wholeheartedly encourage this.

To me, spirituality relates to the process of personal transformation and tapping into our ultimate purpose. Life is meant to be experienced, and we Goddesses are meant to stamp everything we do in this life with our soul signature. If a physical self-inking signature stamp were made for use in recognizing our spiritual accomplishments, an apt expression for it would be, "I am being."

For me, spirituality also means being interconnected with all living beings. Evolving spiritually involves personal growth and transformation. It means paying attention to the beauty of our environment and the people within it, and focusing on the positive side of behaviors or situations.

Your spiritual journey will be uniquely your own, based on your beliefs and the influences others have contributed to your life. Use this chapter to explore and cultivate a unique and loving approach to your own spirituality. Find what works for you, and let the concepts presented provide a creative opening for you to apply and integrate into your individual beliefs and techniques.

According to Dr. Richard P. Johnson, a nationally recognized pioneer in his work related to faith formation in the mature adult, mid-life is the time that our true spiritual development begins to take root. With this innate call to own our wisdom comes the desire to strengthen our spiritual foundation. Through my own experience and research, I have found this to be true. Many women discover that having a spiritual foundation gives them the fortitude to deal with the challenges they are facing in the prime of their lives.

During my first 50+ years, I didn't give much thought to spirituality or looking within. When I was first told a number of years ago during an intuitive reading that I was a very spiritual person, I was quite surprised. I came home and did some research to see what this might mean. Like many, I had some misconstrued ideas of what spirituality entailed, falsely considering it synonymous with religion.

As you read in this chapter's Goddess story, for many women this spiritual foundation is not rooted in any particular religion; it is soul-based. It is about their inner personal growth and the resulting transformation this brings about. It is about their expanded views on what is important to them, and the person they are becoming. They have had enough "doing" – now it's about being!

You may have felt a longing for more bliss, peace, and meaning in your life. In my own life, it seemed as though out of the blue I was receiving subtle messages of unrest and the need for change. These messages started to occur more often and provided the impetus for my spiritual exploration. Pay attention to these pivotal moments and carefully consider how to respond to these callings, which are really profound guidance.

Spirituality surrounds us in everything we do. It touches the internal part of us that is not dependent on material things or physical comforts. Spirituality is not about what we have or what we do, but how we relate to everything – our relationships, our work, our obligations, our lives. Having a spiritual foundation helps us live well with those around us. This foundation is what guides us to live with integrity and purpose and seek serenity and joy in life. Acknowledging our spirituality also contributes to finding meaning and purpose. It teaches us how to find the elements that are weak or missing, such as inner peace and self-love.

Here are just some of the **benefits of spiritual living**:

- Reflects internal wealth
- Promotes the ability to form deeper connections with others
- Teaches us about spending our time on things of real value
- Promotes better mental health and supports stress reduction
- Promotes mindful living – not living in a fog of "always doing"
- Teaches us how to live harmoniously in our world
- Nourishes our heart and soul
- Guides us to find who we truly are and encourages personal growth
- Gives us the permission to pause and reflect
- Inspires us to regularly practice self-compassion
- Supports us in more graciously accepting our ever-evolving physical body

Much of my personal growth has taken place on the spiritual level. Through my journey and the resulting transformation, I have developed a growing awareness of the purpose and meaning of life. I am now living my life based on my personal mission statement, which has developed from my current core values, passions, and dreams. My business vision and values also mirror my personal ones. Achieving congruency in life is how we find hope, joy, and inner peace, all of which bring us back to our natural state of happiness.

Yes, this is our *natural state* and not something we find – believe me, I tried searching for it and came full circle, learning I had it inside me all along.

Being In the Now

One of the most basic, yet difficult strategies to employ when we want to start living a clear, spiritual life is focusing on the present moment. This is often called "being in the now," being present with whatever is happening in each moment, without judgment. When we are connected with what is true for us in the present moment, we are no longer trapped by the negative emotions generated by troublesome memories or worries. We can return to a state of peace and serenity, with the truth of the experience in front of us in every moment.

 There is an old saying – take time to smell the roses! Life is too short not to appreciate the beauty of it.

About three years ago, I started my quest to find what was missing from my life. I met Ian, a very successful businessman who had left the corporate world to embark on his own spiritual journey. Ian established a support group for others who wanted to make a difference in the world. It was a diverse, passionate, and cohesive "mastermind" group for exchanging and developing ideas.

At one memorable meeting with just a handful of attendees present, Ian asked each person what they were working on and where they needed help. Some synergistic sharing took place. Certainly some goals with soul were formulated that night. He spoke about "being in the now" and the other heads nodded affirmatively. Then he noted the blank stare on my face and took a step back to ask if everyone understood this phrase, knowing full well I did not.

Ian led us through an exercise so we could experience the concept in action. In groups of two, we sat across the table from one another and were instructed to stare into the eyes of our partner, a virtual stranger. For five minutes we focused only on them and gazed deeply into their eyes. Blinking was permitted; talking was not.

Those five minutes felt like an eternity. At first, I heard all the background noises that surrounded me, people coughing, or traffic from the outside. I felt uncomfortable. However, when I concentrated on gazing deeply into the other person's eyes, a sense of peace and "mindfulness" took over and I truly understood the power of "being in the now." My eyes welled up. You may have heard the old saying, "The eyes are the window to the soul." In that moment, I personally experienced the truth of that expression.

I later learned this exercise (called "eye-gazing") is commonly used to increase intimacy between partners or strangers. This was a helpful introduction to my understanding of what it truly means to be in the now. It is about being as present as we can, in every situation. For me, being present means slowing down and savoring life's moments.

Blossom and Transform

> "Spiritual blossoming simply means blossoming in life in all dimensions, being happy, at ease with yourself and with everybody around you." *Sri Sri*

We Goddesses have a deep-rooted need to express ourselves in our own unique and soulful way, which allows us to blossom and transform like a budding rose, or a caterpillar transforming into a monarch butterfly. If that gift of personal expression is taken from us, we become starved souls, full of so much pain that we stagnate and wither.

 Remember: the goal is to blossom and transform, not stagnate and wither!

Spirituality is the touchstone that keeps us connected. Attuning to our highest self allows us to know when we are off-track, and deepening our spiritual practice helps us get back on track more quickly over time.

Yes, we want to be who we are meant to be – uniquely ourselves – but sometimes we need support. We need connections with others in order to thrive in all ways, including spiritually. But our friends and family may not be in the same headspace or able to support us in expanding on our spiritual foundation. If this is the position you are in, I encourage you to look for a meet-up group (www.meetup.com) in your area. For instance, you might enter the word "spirituality" to find a group of like-minded people. We all have stories to tell, and can benefit from telling our stories and listening to the stories of others. In doing so, we share the accumulated wisdom, further advancing our personal growth and expanding our spiritual self.

The opportunity of exploring our spirituality can support us in making the rest of our life the best of our life. There is so much more of life to be experienced and expressed. How do you do this? By *being* more and *feeling* more while you are here.

One of the key elements of spirituality is looking *within*, so that is where we will go in the next chapter.

Chapter 4

Looking Within

"One of the most courageous things you can do is **identify with yourself, know who you are, what you believe in**, and where you want to go."
Sheila Murray Bethel

Goddess Tenet #3: A Goddess trusts her intuition and continues to tap into this powerful source of guidance to support her needs.

Goddess Sue, age 54, from Auckland, New Zealand tells her story:

My awareness came to me around the age of seven. I became more aware that I was not like everyone else. I would hear voices and ask, "Who's there?" only to find that I was alone. I was constantly teased for this, and so I began to ignore these voices as much as I could.

My fondest moment of this "knowing" was when my late Nana came to visit me – only this was no ordinary visit. I knew at an early age that my Nana "got" me. She knew what went on inside my head. My Nana and I always had a magic bond when she was alive, and this bond seemed to transcend the physical limitations of life and death.

We had just returned home on a ferry after Nana's Tangi (a funeral rite of the Maori people). It had been a long day. I climbed into bed, said goodnight to my family, and fell fast asleep. I still don't know if I was awake or heard the steps in my dream, but I heard the familiar sound of my Nana walking up our drive – something that always made me happy. I could hear her walking up all 15 steps to the front door. I heard the door open and close, and then she walked into my bedroom. The light went on and I remember thinking/dreaming/wondering what she was doing there at that time of night. I was aware it was late. Nana came to my bedside, stroked my face, and said, "She's fine, now – that's good."

I often wondered if she had done this to all my siblings – there are seven of us. I never ever spoke about this to them, because they were part of the teasings. I vividly remember lying there, wanting to say something to her, but I couldn't move or speak. I was frozen, and she left. No steps, no walking, just gone. The light was actually on and I had to get up to turn it off. To this day, no one in my family claims to have done it. I believe it was Nana's way of saying, "It was real, you did see me."

While we were away from home at her Tangi, Nana came to the house where the children had to sleep, while the adults prepared for the feast and wake after the burial. We were all asleep on the mattresses in the lounge of my auntie's house and Nana came to the doorway of the lounge. She scanned the room with the biggest smile, looking at all her grandkids, and then was gone.

From then on, I found I was able to make predictions – small things at first, mostly who was having a baby next. I became aware of other people's energy. I would feel whether or not I liked a person, and was very accurate with who was a good person and who was not. For instance, my Auntie had a male friend I disliked from day one. He went on to sexually abuse me.

For a long time I had no faith in myself. I doubted my value and didn't know what clairvoyance, spirituality, and the like meant. I continued to see and hear things and, as crazy as it was, I continued hiding it from everyone until I was in my 30s. Between then and my 51st year of life, so much self-awareness developed, it was amazing. I began to talk to people and realized what I had was a gift. I began feeling happy to share experiences. The more I shared, the more like-minded people came into my life. I no longer felt alone or different, and reclaimed the term "weird." It was a term I had always hated, but I now wore proudly like a neon badge.

Relief is what we all seek – relief from pain, relief from stress – but a lot of us accept things we shouldn't as "our lot" in life. I now know it is not our lot in life; it is just a string of events that make up our life. But we can change all of them just by changing the way we look at them. We can see them as opportunities to choose something different, or as examples of what we don't want more of, and then shift our focus to what we do want.

While in my late 40s and early 50s, I have earned certifications in many things. I am now a Law of Attraction life coach, a Reiki master and Reiki master teacher, an Angel card reader, and a Light Body graduate. All of these life tools became known to me when I discovered Law of Attraction coaching. I had no idea it would have anything to do with spirituality. Now I know my soul was leading me to a place to fill all the gaps in this part of the book of my life. This spiritual journey was not without a map.

I now have many close friends who share these gifts, and have recently discovered my four children do as well.

* * *

The more we acknowledge our spirituality and work on being present in every experience, the closer we become to our higher selves. Sue is an example of someone who was able to access this connection naturally and easily; for others, it takes time, patience, and practice to achieve that level of attunement. What Sue experienced is possible for all of us, if we cultivate our intuition. This is best done by looking within.

When we cannot hear our inner wisdom, we become misaligned. This contributes to creativity blockages, various negative health manifestations, self-confidence and self-esteem issues, and relationship conflicts, as well as other less than ideal behaviors and feelings. However, from time to time – and this is that time – we need to pause and quench our thirst by taking a nurturing gulp from the deep well of feminine wisdom we possess. It's time to awaken and embrace our true inner potential and the powerful Goddess within.

As females on a journey to living a life of fulfillment and purpose, we need to recapture our identities and reclaim our feminine energy. It is commonly believed that as we have made our way into the corporate world (traditionally perceived to be the domain of men), we have downplayed many of our feminine qualities and adopted masculine qualities thought necessary for success. It is crucial that we reclaim those feminine characteristics. They are paramount to our returning to wholeness, as they represent our very identity. What we have lost does not just affect us; it perpetuates a loss of balance in the larger world, as well, because feminine energy is so critically important to humanity.

We need to reconnect with our feminine qualities of gentleness, tenderness, and collaboration – to encourage a nurturing environment within which love can flourish. Most importantly, we need to direct some of that love toward ourselves.

Getting in Touch with Our Intuition

"You must train your intuition. You must trust the small voice inside which tells you exactly what to say, what to decide." *Ingrid Bergman*

Another feminine aspect with which many of us have lost touch is our gift of intuition. Intuition – that small voice inside of us that tells us the truth – is the part of our being that is open to receiving the information our heart and mind send our way. When we live spiritually, with attention to being in the now, and are able to be in stillness each day, we are able to access our highest self, the self most attuned with our intuition.

Many of us have allowed that voice that quietly guides us toward what is true and what is most important to get drowned out. Rather than getting to know our highest self and loving her unconditionally, we have lost touch with our intuition in the hectic pace of our busy lives, or in trying to be all things to all people, which inhibits our personal growth. Experts in intuitive counseling say we can learn to develop our intuition and use those insights to guide us in our personal healing. Just like meditation, developing our intuition takes practice.

Consider the following questions:

- Do you believe your intuition gives you good advice most of the time?
- Do you take your body's early warning signs (and the accompanying intuitive thoughts) seriously and seek medical advice?
- Do you listen to your intuition when it warns you about a new person you are meeting?
- Do you listen to the intuitive messages brought to you through your dreams?

More than likely you answered *yes* to at least one of these questions. If so, here are four ways to strengthen your intuition:

1. **Trust your instincts:** Do your homework – but when you have leveled the playing field and the options are equal, trust your intuition to make your decision.
2. **Trust your first response**: We have all heard the good advice of not changing our test answers, as our first response is more often than not the correct response. This can be applied to anything in life.
3. **Journal:** Document your intuitive thoughts in your journal and then look back to determine how many times your

instincts were right. This is a good way to watch your intuition develop.

4. **Meditate**: Meditation helps clear our mind of repetitive thoughts and worries, making it easier to focus on our intuitive thoughts.

Mindfulness

"The most fundamental aggression to ourselves, the most fundamental harm we can do ourselves, is to remain ignorant by not having the courage and the respect to look at ourselves honestly and gently."
Pema Chödrön

Meditation and mindfulness practice go hand in hand. My meditation practice is what allows me to be mindful and "in the now" each day. If you fill every moment of every day with activities, unrelenting busy-ness *does not a happy Goddess make*. Unless we learn about and practice mindfulness, we will continue to be stuck in this rushed, stressed, unsettled – and ultimately unhappy – lifestyle so many of us currently live. We will continue to spin in a vortex of *doing,* leaving little or no time for simply *being*.

When you practice mindfulness, you are in a state of alert and focused relaxation. Once you are in this state, the key is to pay attention to the thoughts you are thinking, in a non–judgmental way. The goal is to let the thoughts go and refocus on the present moment. Allow thoughts to enter, and then let them pass without judgment. It is worth the effort. Studies have identified mindfulness as a key component in happiness.[10]

---

[10] Shapiro, S.L. (2009) Meditation and Positive Psychology. In Eds: S.J. Lopez & C.R. Snyder, Oxford Handbook of Positive Psychology. NY: Oxford University Press

Meditation

> "Meditation is not a way of making your mind quiet. It's a way of entering into the quiet that's already there – buried under the 65,000 thoughts the average person thinks every day." *Deepak Chopra*

Meditation is a mind-body practice that results in increased calmness and a state of physical relaxation. Meditation can be a wonderful tool to help us get in touch with our inner selves. Despite what many people think, meditation is not a religious practice. It is practiced by people of different faiths, as well as those with no religious affiliation.

Along with being an essential practice for those interested in cultivating mindfulness, meditation is often used as a complementary and alternative medicinal option. Meditation enhances our coping skills. It has both positive psychological and spiritual benefits.

Psychological Benefits

- Helps us control our thoughts
- Promotes self-confidence
- Enhances concentration and focus
- Increases levels of serotonin (a chemical produced by the brain, which helps with mood regulation)
- Helps resolve phobias and fears
- Supports creativity
- Develops intuition

Spiritual Benefits

- Supports keeping things in perspective
- Promotes a deeper understanding of self and others
- Increases compassion for ourselves and others
- Helps us discover our true purpose

- Provides peace of mind and happiness
- Promotes harmony of mind, body, and spirit
- Aids in an increased acceptance of oneself

Meditation brings us the opportunity to be quiet and still, and helps us cultivate a state of inner peace. The best part is that even a small amount of time each day will bring benefits, and (as with all the best things in life) it is free.

 ## Exercise: Meditation

At this point you may be thinking, "This all sounds well and good, but I don't know how to meditate." A simple technique is to pay attention to the breath. There is no wrong way to do this. Much like training our body through exercise, following our breath trains our mind to be fully relaxed and silent, thus strengthening concentration and encouraging a state of inner peace.

Here are six easy steps to help you get started in your meditation practice:

1. Find a quiet spot in your home that is free from distractions.
2. Sit in a comfortable chair, with your back straight and eyes closed.
3. Pay attention to your breathing. Listen to it and follow it. As you breathe from your abdomen, repeat a word or phrase silently to yourself. I use the phrase "in breath" when I inhale and "out breath" as I exhale; or sometimes I use the phrase "love and compassion for me" as I inhale and "love and compassion for others" during my exhalation.
4. When your mind wanders – *and it will* – just notice it and bring your attention back to your breath. Remember, "in breath," and, "out breath," or whatever phrase you choose to use.
5. Set aside time each day to practice. Morning is easiest, but if clearing your head through the sanctuary of meditation in the

middle of a busy day works best for you, that's fine, too. Some prefer to meditate at the end of their day, as well.

6.   Start practicing meditation for 5-15 minutes per day, at least 4-5 times per week, to garner the full benefits.

Thousands of thoughts pass through our minds daily, so meditation does take some practice – but so does anything worthwhile we want to become proficient at. Keep at it; the rewards are worth the effort.

Journaling

"Whatever it is that you write, putting words on the page is a form of therapy that doesn't cost a dime, and it is certainly a productive way to deal with the scars and dark places from our pasts. Self-expression is one way to lay a problem or demon to rest. It's also a way to bring forth suppressed feelings and fears. It's a way to bring a sense of resolution and a sense of satisfaction to our lives." *Diana Raab*

Journaling on a daily basis can be a liberating and empowering exercise that brings us closer to the wisdom of our intuition. Importantly, it provides an opportunity to reflect. Self-awareness is the key to keeping us moving forward, and will encourage us to think more deeply. Thus, the act of writing helps us solve the complex issues that challenge us, in the face of dilemmas and contradictory thoughts; and documenting our personal thoughts, daily experiences, and evolving insights is a powerful way to discover ourselves.

Journaling also creates an opportunity to document and track our personal and professional goals.[11] Writing down these goals yields a higher success rate in achieving them than not documenting them.

---

[11]   http://www.huffingtonpost.com/thai-nguyen/benefits-of-journaling-_b_6648884.html

Think about the times when you've made a *to do* list. Did more things got accomplished when you did this?

Moreover, journaling about stressful and painful events and emotions helps to reduce the intensity of these feelings. This helps us come to terms with them more quickly, thereby reducing their long-term impact on our mental[12] and physical health.[13] This allows us to feel calmer and, if done daily, provides us with a self-prescribed regular boost of self-focus, which promotes us staying in the present, as opposed to dwelling on the past.

 Remember: what you resist persists!

Last but not least, journaling provides a creative and therapeutic outlet. It enables us to access our analytical, rational "left" brain, leaving our "right" brain open to be creative, intuitive, and thoughtful. So, in a sense, writing can take you out of your head and bring you closer to your heart.[14] Journaling allows us to use all our brain power to help us better understand ourselves.

 Journaling Exercise

Now that you know some of the valuable benefits, here are five simple steps you can use to begin your journaling practice:

1. Purchase a journal. Choose a cover that resonates with you on some level. To get you started, there is a selection of journals available through Amazon at: www.TransformingVenus. com/product-category/inner-transformation/journals/

---

[12] https://www.urmc.rochester.edu/encyclopedia/content.aspx?Content TypeID=1&ContentID=4552

[13] Purcell, M. (2013). The Health Benefits of Journaling. *Psych Central*. Retrieved on February 27, 2016, from http://psychcentral.com/lib/the-health-benefits-of-journaling/

[14] https://theheartofawakening.wordpress.com/tag/life/

Alternatively, you may choose to use an electronic journal on your computer. I would suggest you password-protect your file to ensure your privacy.

2. Find a peaceful, quiet spot where you will not be interrupted and where you feel safe to document your innermost thoughts.

3. Find a practice you associate with relaxation and preface your journaling with this ritual. For instance, you might have a relaxing cup of tea, take a bubble bath, perform a short meditation, have a glass of wine, or burn a scented candle or incense.

4. Start each entry by documenting the date and time.

5. Aim to spend 15-20 minutes each day writing down whatever thoughts come into your mind, especially your deeper thoughts pertaining to things that are bothering you, with deeper reflection on the *why*.

At the end of each day, document a response to these three questions, along with any other words that reflect how your soul was touched that day:

1. What was my most life-giving experience today?
2. What was my most life-draining experience today?
3. What small or big step did I take today to bring me closer to living a spiritual life?

By responding to these three questions, your consciousness will expand and you will quickly see what you need to let go of because it is not energy-giving; it is energy-draining. You will also see what life-giving experiences you should be focusing on, instead.

Trusting your inner wisdom, your intuition, and your heart will permit your inner voice to emerge and will create a new sense of self-awareness that will provide unlimited growth potential.

Chapter 5

The Power of Positivity and Inspirational Thoughts

"I am as close to changing my life as my current positive thought." *Louise L. Hay*

Goddess Tenet #11: A Goddess is a generous, joyful being who understands the paramount importance of gratitude and positivity, and expresses these on a daily basis.

Goddess Tanya, age 51, from Saskatchewan, Canada tells her story:

I have just turned 51 and never felt more comfortable with myself, more in tune with my inner voice, or more alive. And I'm just getting started. But it certainly hasn't always been that way.

Despite many challenges, insecurities, introversion, and lack of confidence, I have always been an optimist. That optimism has grown as I've gotten older and developed me into a positive, grateful person. That has helped me on my journey.

It certainly helped in 2008 when our world fell apart. Just like that, our jobs and security were gone. There had been signs that we needed to make changes in our lives, but we didn't pay attention at the time. We hit rock bottom.

The good news about hitting rock bottom is that there is nowhere to go but up. We realized we needed to uproot and start fresh.

After our "crash," we moved to a small, quiet, rural town we never thought we would ever move to! As we settled into a new routine of simpler lives and rebuilding, we were warned that the town was "cliquey" and full of gossip, and that our daughter would have trouble with the kids in her grade, as the local kids had been trouble since their early years. One person who had lived in this town most of their life even asked me, "Why the hell would you ever want to live here?"

I had to find a coping mechanism and at that moment I chose optimism, without fully understanding how powerful that choice would be. It ended up changing everything – what I saw, what I did, how I reacted, how I embraced life. Much to everyone's surprise, the small town we moved to ended up being one of the best moves we ever made. Three weeks into school, I asked our daughter how things were going and I will never forget her words: "Mom, it feels as though I have lived here my whole life."

For me, I decided to get back into Health Care after being out of the field for several years. I never thought I would go back to it and before long, I remembered why I had left: it didn't make me happy. I remember sitting in my vehicle before work in the mornings, crying. Then I would regroup and walk through that door. In retrospect, the opportunities and experiences I had while working there are what prompted me to start my own business, and for that, I am so grateful.

I vividly remember driving to another small town for a board meeting. It was an early spring morning, too early to be driving; the sun was barely up. This was going to be such a long day. "Why am I here? How did this happen? I'm not sure I like this. In fact, I don't really like anything." That dialogue in my head caused my heart to race, my palms to sweat, and the tears to start. There was no way I could function in a meeting.

I pulled over to the shoulder of the road and turned off the car. Then

I turned off the radio. I rolled down the window, sat in silence, and looked. I looked up and I saw. Right then, as the full sun shone on the rolling wheat fields just beginning to grow, I had the realization that I had never truly noticed how blue the sky was next to the green fields. I noticed how beautiful everything was all around me, and I had never really seen any of it before.

While in my state of chaos (a state I had created), I had been blind to these moments of wonder that are always available. Now, I took it all in, my moment of awakening. I started the car, left the window down, left the radio off, got to that board meeting, and rocked some awesome! This was the beginning of realizing the power I had to change my experiences. I was beginning to feel like a new person.

A few days prior to that, I had been driving to a nearby city, again crying. I remember feeling as if everything was in slow motion, wipers going back and forth. I was listening to a CD and a dance mix of "Long Train Running" by The Doobie Brothers started playing. Don't ask me where this epiphany came from, but I thought, "I am going to dance to that song on stage one day!" I had never taken dance lessons, but our three daughters had. While I would proudly watch them in performances, I would think, "Please God, in my next life, let me be a dancer."

A few days later, I received a phone call from my lovely aunt. "Tanya," she said, "you need to come and check out this amazing class."

"It's OK," I said.

"It's the most fun I've had."

"No, I'm good."

"Just come to one class!"

"Yeah, sure."

Well, that class was Zumba and my aunt was right; it was the most fun I'd had in a long time. Before long, my aunt and I decided to train as Zumba instructors. We took as many training sessions as we could, across a few provinces and when funds would allow. Eight months later, I was on a stage in that beautiful town I lived in, with 48 beautiful smiling women looking at me, ready to dance and have fun.

The first song I played? The dance mix of "Long Train Running" by The Doobie Brothers!

Were these times hard? – check.

Took small steps – check.

Celebrated small steps – check.

Embraced change – check.

Got involved – check.

Looked for the positives in our new life – check.

Had hard moments – check.

Remained optimistic – check.

Met amazing friends – check.

Life-changing – check.

My message to you is about creating positive change, the power of optimism, changing your story, shifting your thoughts, and taking action. I am proof that these strategies work. There will always be people who don't understand as you make changes in your life, and that's okay. Some may be people you were once close to. Bless them and carry on. You will form many new relationships as you go on your new journey. Remember the first relationship is with you. When you find your own unique way to shine and live your best life – please trust me on this – you give others permission to do so, as well, however that may look for them. We are all on separate journeys. It all starts with believing you can – and that, my friend, is absolutely free.

I have a lot of good living left to do, and you, beautiful soul, do as well. I believe in me and I believe in YOU. Let's get out there and dance!

It is never ever too late to find your calling, discover your passion, reinvent yourself, learn to love yourself, rethink, redo, start over, face your fears, and live your own best life. I am proof of that.

* * *

Page by page and chapter by chapter, we have been on a journey. We have been making an effort to reflect on our personal life situation, to determine what is holding us back and what we are missing. We recognize that only harmful negative effects will manifest from having an unhealthy critical relationship with self. We realize that to move forward, we must stray from the status quo and develop a healthy, empowering personal relationship with our self. We realize that where our focus goes, energy flows, and we are tired of feeding that negative energy.

Michael Bernard Beckwith, the spiritual leader of the Agape International Spiritual Center in Santa Monica, California, is known for his saying, "A bad day for the ego is a good day for the soul." We want more good days for our soul! We didn't sign up for *this* (restless and stuck) – we are looking for *bliss*, and we want to have the starring role in our own life! We want to flourish, we want to be happy, and despite what some of the negative Nellys in your life have told you – we can have it all!

One way to boost our bliss is to cultivate more positive thoughts. For example, I created my Facebook page as a way of contributing more positivity in the world. As I started to find and share positive inspirational thoughts, and receive kind feedback from my growing number of followers, I knew I was on the right path. I began to pay attention to things I had previously taken for granted. Awareness is a wonderful thing. Have you ever noticed when you are in the market for a major purchase, you start to notice every detail about that purchase? For instance, if you are shopping for a new front door, you suddenly notice all the front doors in your neighborhood; everywhere you go, you look at everyone else's doors, and you focus on the ones you see in magazines and on TV. When I started to focus on and share positive empowering messages with other women on my Facebook page, *I* felt more positive and empowered. I became more aware of positive inspirational happenings. When I found them, I shared them. You may go see for yourself at www.facebook.com/ TransformingVenus. I call them Goddess Gems.

Positive interactions are everywhere. For instance, I was traveling in another country and I was short a few dollars in that country's currency to pay for my purchase. The teenager in line behind me insisted on making up the difference. When I shared this message on my Facebook page, others shared similar positive experiences from their own lives. Once, I posted a message about every person touching your life for a reason, and over 100 women responded with a message supporting this positive thought. These are just a few examples of how our positive energy has a rippling effect, drawing in even more positive energy.

A positive person will take every step in life with purpose and see every moment as an opportunity – a growth opportunity, an opportunity to smile or laugh, an opportunity to experience something new. They even see failure as an opportunity to learn.

Here's a powerful example:

In 2006, a Kansas City minister named Will Bowen challenged his congregation to stop complaining about lack for 21 days. He gave them each a bracelet they were to move from one wrist to the other each time they noted a complaint, an inherently negative thought, passing through their minds. Those who could last the full three weeks without the need to move their bracelet between wrists would be issued a certificate of happiness. Bowen claimed the negativity of complaining "[is] like bad breath – you notice it when it comes out of everyone else's mouth, but not your own." This simple lesson went viral, and A Complaint-Free World – a non-profit, non-religious organization – has now distributed over ten million bracelets to individuals throughout 106 countries in the world, with the ultimate goal of effecting positive change in the world.[15]

We all have work to do in decreasing the number of complaints and negative thoughts that drift through our minds on a daily basis. We all face challenges in reaching this goal. In today's media-driven, device-oriented society, bad news travels faster than ever before. When we hear tragic stories, we often feel the need to share them with everyone. The negative thoughts that prevail with this bad news can become an obsession. It narrows our perspectives, preventing us from being open-minded and rational. Think of a time you have been in a heated disagreement with someone. Your emotions and anger more than likely blinded you from seeing the other person's perspective.

---

[15] http://www.willbowen.com/

Negative thoughts and perceptions are not necessarily in alignment with the truth, and these can make up a big part of negative self-talk. Perhaps you haven't been eating healthily or exercising on a regular basis. Your negative self-talk may sound like this: *I'm lazy, I lack motivation and willpower, I'm so far out of shape, this isn't worth working at,* and on and on. Sound familiar? This is blatantly untrue. Perhaps you don't know where to start and just need some support, or perhaps time is an issue and you need suggestions to help organize your busy lifestyle. In these scenarios, the negative self-talk accomplishes nothing but a drain on your energy, which keeps you stuck.

Bad things do and will continue to happen; this is a part of life. I am not suggesting you bury your head in the sand; I'm simply suggesting you make a special effort to cultivate more positivity into your life rather than dwell on the negative. We need to learn to frame our thoughts in a way that supports us. Additionally, the opportunity of learning from challenging experiences is more productive and, therefore, a personally rewarding focus. Studies have proven that positive emotions expand our sense of possibility, opening our minds to seeing countless potential options.

Benefits of Positivity

Positive thinking is commonly correlated with effective stress management. In other words, positive people are better able to cope with stressful situations. Instead of dwelling on the undesired circumstances, the positive individual is more likely to develop a plan to ensure similar situations in the future result in better outcomes. For example, if they did not get hired for a job, they might look at the situation as being within their control and put a plan in place to address any skill gaps that might have hindered their first attempt.

Your thoughts also have a powerful effect on your immune system. Cultivating positive energy and maintaining a positive attitude can go a long way in providing a supportive structure that enhances our immune system functions. In August 2002, a study administered by the Mayo Clinic revealed that pessimists scored lower than optimists on their quality of life scale, and on the mental and physical functioning scales.[16] Two years earlier, a separate study concluded that individuals with a more pessimistic or negative view of life demonstrated a 19% increase in the risk of mortality (death).[17]

In 2004, a study published in the *Journal of Research in Personality* looked at the health benefits of writing about an intensely positive experience.[18] All participants were given a writing assignment taking place over three consecutive days. Half of the participants were instructed to write about a really positive experience and the other half were given a control topic. Three months after the writing assignment, health center visits were assessed. The individuals who wrote about the positive experience had significantly fewer visits to the health center than the control group. Even 90 days later, those same individuals showed enhanced positive mood measures in the follow-up assessment. This makes a strong case for picking up a pen and journal to write about your own positive experiences, both from a mood and health perspective.

 The good news is that positive thinking skills can be learned!

Positive and Negative Energy Forces

"People like to be around those who give off positive energy." *Erin Heatherton*

They're out there. I call them energy vampires. They come in many forms, but they all share the same characteristic: they are

---

[16] http://www.mayoclinicproceedings.org/article/S0025-6196(11)62018-1/fulltext

[17] http://www.mayoclinicproceedings.org/article/S0025-6196(11)64184-0/pdf

[18] Burton, C.M., & King, L.A. (2004). The health benefits of writing about intensely positive experiences. *Journal of Research in Personality*, 38, 150-163

"takers." I'm sure you have people like this in your life. Think of the sob sister, who always feels sorry for herself and wants everyone else to come along for the ride; the manipulative one, who always tries to get you to follow his/her agenda; the drama queen, where something is always going wrong in her life. The list goes on.

Energy vampires think the world revolves around them and cannot seem to find any positivity in their life. They feel the need to share every sad saga with those who will listen. Most energy vampires are just unhappy individuals who latch onto and feed on the precious energy of others by sharing the drama in their lives, which is typically blown way out of proportion.

Energy vampires can leave you feeling depleted, upset, weary and, in rare cases, frightened and attacked. If you know someone like this and they are rooted in your life, now is a good time to put a little distance between you and their negativity. If this person is very close to you and distance is not an option, at the very least, put some clear boundaries in place.

We are the guardians of our own energetic space. From this point forward, we need to surround ourselves with more people and situations that radiate positive energy. This is extremely important to support our personal growth and accomplish the goals we set for ourselves. We want to connect with those individuals who are capable of interacting with us, to create synergy. Make sure you foster relationships where you *build on* each other's energy. Spend time with people capable of *giving*. The energy vampire cannot give – not right now. They need to do their own inner work.

Energy fields surround us – both negative and positive. In order to feed our energy levels, we need to learn to embrace the positive and say *no* to the negative. Our bodies and spirits are energy. Energy vibrations radiate from everything that exists: people, pets, nature, everything in the Universe. When we emit positive energy, we attract more positivity into our space – and positive energy is contagious. Think of a sporting event or concert you might attend; everyone in the crowd is on an energy high. Regardless of your mood when you arrive, in that crowd your level of positive energy can't help but rise.

Another example is music. You could be in a bit of a funk, but when a fun, high-energy upbeat song comes on the radio, chances are you'll get swept into a more positive mind space. Or have you ever had a friend who listened to your woes and responded supportively? Didn't you start to feel better and more positive about the situation? In all of these cases, positive energy permeates your space, resulting in an uplifting experience.

Eleven Tips for Cultivating Positivity

Here are eleven explicit tips for cultivating more positive energy in your life.

1. **Surround yourself with positive people.** Make an effort to spend more time with people who exude positive energy and lift you up. They may also provide helpful advice and invite you to see things from a different perspective.

2. **Practice positive self-talk.** Stop being so hard on yourself! Change the flavor and tone of the conversations you have with yourself. With practice, your self-talk will include less criticism and more self-acceptance. Choose to be encouraging and supportive, and treat yourself with the same positive, loving kindness you would impart to a good friend (and yes, become your own best friend).

3. **Choose happiness and find your bliss.** It's up to you – choose happiness. In every moment, you have the choice of refocusing any negative thoughts and replacing them with happy thoughts. Appreciate the blessings – big or small – in your life.

4. **Add more smiles and laughter moments to your day.** When a stranger smiles at you on the street, do you experience a little boost of "feel good"? This is a two-way street; both the giver and the receiver benefit from that moment. Or think about the feel-good moments of having a deep belly laugh.

Laughter really is the best medicine, and the positive energy it generates is contagious.

5. **Share inspirational stories, quotes, and positive affirmations.** You may wish to write a positive and inspirational story of your own in your journal. The Transforming Venus website (www.transformingvenus.com) has a story-sharing page, so you may wish to submit your story for publication to help other women. You can also subscribe and receive a daily Goddess Gem in your inbox, which are inspirational motivational words of wisdom designed to give you a boost. Both options are free, and are offered with the ultimate goal of supporting you in your personal transformation.

6. **Energy is a precious commodity – stop giving your power away!** Each time you focus on negative thoughts, you deplete your precious energy reserves. The healthy alternative is to put your effort into cultivating positivity, and recharge your batteries so you can share your abundant energy with others in need. Think of yourself as a magnet and make it your mission to pull in all the positive energy emitted from the world around you, allowing you to shine like a beacon. Others will follow your light, allowing them to see the benefits of cultivating their own positive energy.

7. **Develop an attitude of gratitude.** Gratitude is a key component in shifting your mindset. When you can be grateful even for the things that do not go well in the day, you are truly cultivating a positive mindset. You have many wonderful qualities and traits for which you may wish to express gratitude. In your journal, consider listing as many of them as you can, and then add to this list as you go on. You may even choose to keep a separate gratitude journal and write in it each morning and/or evening as a way of staying present with the blessings in your life.

8. **The past is history – let it go!** The past serves two purposes – it provides you with memories to reflect upon and offers the

opportunity to learn from previous life lessons. This means you need to disengage yourself from dwelling on situations and disappointments that are yesterday's news, and focus on the here and now. Of course, you can learn from past situations and mistakes, but let the lesson you learned be the take-away and release the re-runs. Give yourself permission to move forward.

9. **Meditate.** Those who meditate on a daily basis emit more positive energy than those who do not. The practice of meditation has been highlighted as a valuable practice throughout this book to support a host of personal growth undertakings. I encourage everyone to begin meditating. The benefits truly are profound.

10. **Use creative visualizations.** Creative visualization is an exercise where you use your imagination to picture your wants and desires as if they already exist in reality. When you change your thoughts and the mental images within your mind, you change your reality. As an experiment, consider a situation you are facing right now. Now visualize a highly positive outcome for that situation – the *best*-case scenario. Perhaps you are struggling with a health issue and awaiting some potentially frightening test results. Instead of expecting dire news, visualize positive results or picture a positive treatment outcome. Picture yourself moving forward with your life in perfect health. Focusing on what we don't want is energy-absorbing. Instead, focus on positive thoughts, such as what makes you feel good. There are many examples of individuals who have healed themselves through the power of positive energy – their own and the energy of others!

11. **Schedule in a play day.** We Goddesses know how to schedule; we have appointments at work, household responsibilities, school meetings, children's sporting and school events, travel, appointments, and a host of other functions in our daily calendars – but we often neglect to

schedule time to *relax*. When was the last time you put some time aside to explore and experience something new – or put up your feet – or just have *fun?* If you have to rack your brain for a response, I challenge you to make more time for yourself. Make a picnic lunch and invite a friend on an excursion, go to the park and swing on a swing, put on some music and dance around your living room, build a sand castle at the beach, go on a nature walk, skip, juggle a couple of oranges, color, create your dream board *(discussed in chapter 16)*, teach a child a new game – whatever you've been wanting to do, start doing it *now*.

Affirmations

One of the most effective ways to bring positivity to your mind is the use of affirmations. Affirmations are statements that affirm the feeling of already having what you desire. A simple way to start working with affirmations is to write a series of "I am" statements describing how you want to feel. They should be written as if you have already achieved this feeling. Write them with a positive intonation, in the present tense, and include an intention or belief. Make sure your affirmations resonate with you, and put some passion and feeling into them.

Here are a few examples to help you get started:

- I am <u>competent, smart, and full of Goddess wisdom</u>.
- I am <u>open to continued growth and development to support my transformation</u>.
- I am <u>absolutely good enough; in fact, I am so much more than that</u>.
- I am _____.
- I am _____.

You can work with affirmations by either repeating them out loud while looking in the mirror for five minutes daily, or by thinking them silently to yourself, perhaps repeatedly as you go to sleep. You may also write them in your journal.

The repetition of affirmations, and really feeling the emotions that would accompany the desired outcome, is what make them such a powerful tool. Repeating affirmations consciously gives your subconscious mind a pattern to follow. Positive affirmations are a tool we can use to re-program our subconscious thoughts. And just like meditation, they are simple to use and free. But they only work if you are consistent in your approach and have a true desire to change your present circumstances.

Once you write down your affirmations, it's a good idea to make yourself a few portable print copies. You can keep a copy in your purse to pull out and review during work breaks or while waiting for appointments, and perhaps keep a copy on your nightstand to read before going to sleep. Give that subconscious part of your mind that never shuts off something to do while you get your Goddess beauty rest.

Throughout the rest of the book, each chapter will wrap up with positive affirmations relating to the chapter subject.

Cultivating Positivity: *Right Here, Right Now* Challenge

Respond to the questions below.

1. In order to cultivate more positivity in my life, I chose tip number _____ from the 11 tips previously noted in this chapter to apply to my life at this moment in time.
2. I chose this option for the following reason(s):

   _____
   _____
   _____

3. In order to use this tool to cultivate more positivity into my life, I plan to take the following action steps:

   i. _____

   _____

   ii. _____

   _____

   iii. _____

   _____

4. I will know I have made a difference in raising my level of positivity based on the following indicators (feelings, factors, feedback from others, etc.):

   _____

   _____

   _____

   _____

Once you have documented a response to questions 1-4 and have put the steps outlined in question 3 into practice, come back to this exercise and complete these final reflection pieces to evaluate your success.

5. Reflect on any changes you and others have noticed related to your level of positivity.
   I have noticed:

   _____

   _____

   _____

   _____

   Others have noticed:

   _____

   _____

   _____

   _____

6. Reflect on how you feel about the new level of positive energy you are radiating and the benefits you have noted in your life.

_____

_____

_____

_____

When you are ready challenge yourself to tackle a second tip following the same steps, which you can complete in your journal.

 ## Positive Affirmations Related to Cultivating Positivity and Inspirational Thoughts:

- My thoughts are infused with positivity and my life is abundant in every way.
- Today, I let go of my old thoughts and habits and initiate new healthy, positive ones.
- I am conquering my ailments with new sources of positive energy.
- I go out of my way to cultivate and share inspirational thoughts.

Chapter 6

Choosing the Right Mindset

"The Universe will never force a mindset on you. You have complete free agency to choose fear and suffer unnecessarily if you want to." *Kimberly Giles*

Goddess Tenet #2: A Goddess is an evolutionary being who recognizes her responsibility to continue to learn and grow, both intellectually and spiritually.

Goddess Stella, age 47, from California, United States tells her story:

When it comes to facing my fears, I sometimes need to be hit with a baseball bat before slowing down to recognize and acknowledge them. Facing fears around being a parent was no exception. At the core of my beliefs was an underlying conviction that 1) I could not keep my children safe and 2) who I was wasn't good enough. And I set out to find evidence of these beliefs, rather than question their source, which was related to my own childhood.

I continued living this unquestioned legacy. As a single parent and primary caregiver, my fear of not being able to keep my children safe from the world was so great that I missed the part about keeping them safe from themselves. My fears of them not making wise choices and pulling away from me came to fruition when my daughter began a journey of depression, cutting, and overdosing with prescriptions. She preferred to check out than live her teenage years with a hysterical, over-protective, non-trusting mom. I had become her worst nightmare and my worst fear was no longer limited to my imagination.

I had to acknowledge that I was parenting from fear. Once I did that, I could make another choice, one that would serve me to create the life I wanted. This new approach required diligence and discipline. No longer could I parent on autopilot. I had to become curious about my responses and knee-jerk reactions. I also had to commit to living in the present and using the past as a teacher, rather than a road map. Coming face to face with my daughter's acts of self-harm forced me to step back and look at the big picture. I knew if I did what I had always done, I would get what I had always gotten, just like the famous Einstein quote: "The definition of insanity is doing the same thing over and over again and expecting different results."

Einstein is also known for saying, "We cannot solve a problem on the level of consciousness that it was created." And I have taken his wisdom to heart. I could not solve a problem created in my mind with fear. I had to commit to doing it differently. And that is exactly what I did.

Instead of focusing on everything that was wrong or not perfect or what I didn't want, I chose to move forward, to create a vision of what I did want, and no longer entertain thoughts of doubt or negative self-talk. I had to let go of the stories that anchored my beliefs about what kind of parent I was or, for that matter, the kind I needed to be. I created a space to stand in the parent I am when I am being both brave and vulnerable, when I am no longer looking for or predicting suffering or creating worst-case scenarios. I refused to follow the thoughts that brought me more of what I didn't want and began focusing on the gratitude I have for all that I get to experience as a mom. I no longer felt *the impulse to manipulate the world for my safety. This shift changed everything.*

The daughter who wanted to be as far from me as possible is no longer a stranger in my heart and home. We have boldly redefined our relationship and continue to bring mindfulness to any situation that requires us to look at old patterns and beliefs.

Everything has changed, and all that was required was changing my own mindset.

Mindset

"The greatest discovery of all time is that a person can change his future by merely changing his attitude."
Oprah Winfrey

Our mind is a powerful thing. The stories we tell ourselves and the things we believe about our life, our self, and others can either prevent us from moving forward or allow us to blossom and flourish. In her book entitled *Mindset: The New Psychology of Success*, Stanford University psychologist Dr. Carol Dweck presents years of research on how people achieve and succeed. She states it is related to us having one of two mindsets, which she calls either *fixed* or *growth*.[19] Those who believe they were born with certain talents and abilities, and that is their lot in life, have a fixed mindset. Those with a growth mindset believe that through education, life experience, and perseverance, their talents and abilities will not just develop, but flourish. Those with a growth mindset are committed to moving forward and surround themselves with people who will challenge them and help them grow.

I believe you have a growth mindset, or one in the making, because you are reading this book to help with your transformation. You are on the right track. I challenge you to believe in yourself, erase those

---

[19] Dweck, C. (2008). Mindset: The New Psychology of Success", Ballantine Books Trade Paperback Edition, Random House, New York.

self-limiting doubts, and replace them with positive words, such as, "I can do it," and, "I am ready to tackle this next step." You are capable of achieving so much more. Believe that success is possible and choke out those self-limiting beliefs that are holding you back.

Our thoughts are the foundation of our mindset, so if we want to change our mindset, we have to start by changing our thoughts. The basis of those thoughts includes which mindset we choose, both internally and externally. We can either choose a negative attitude or a positive one.

Our number one priority at all times has to be our frame of mind and keeping the positive energy flowing. Numerous benefits result from having the right frame of mind, as Stella's story demonstrates. With it, we are at our absolute best and can tap into our highest creativity. It is then that things just seem to fall in place and unfold in the most amazing ways.

Since the publication of James Allen's book *As a Man Thinketh* more than a century ago, millions of people around the world have used his positive thinking philosophy to improve their lives in a wide variety of ways including, but not limited to, their health, goal-setting, finding peace, and gaining prosperity. In this book, he introduces us to the concept that we create our reality through our thoughts.[20] *We are what we think* and, therefore, we need to put considerable effort into focusing on thoughts that will nurture and advance us to a higher level of thinking that supports our personal growth. Allen challenges us to see that the thoughts we choose to focus on can either bring us pain and suffering or, alternately, enlighten us and bring great joy.

 I invite all awakening Goddesses to choose enlightening, joyful thoughts that allow them to sparkle and shine!

---

[20] Allen, J. (2007). As a Man Thinketh, Dover Publications.

The Conscious and Subconscious Mind

Our mind can be divided into two distinct components, defined as the "conscious" and the "subconscious." I like to use the "your mind is a garden" analogy to differentiate between these two aspects, as it demonstrates both the growth mindset and the power of positivity all in one short story.

Imagine planting a flower garden; consider this garden *your mind.* We plant the flower seeds in the garden just like we plant *thoughts* in our subconscious mind all day, every day, based on our habitual thought patterns. If our flower garden (subconscious mind) is not well tended, weeds (negative thoughts) will overcome the garden. This creates difficult growing conditions for the beautiful flowers (positive thoughts) to take root and grow. In order to allow a beautiful garden (of positive, growth-inducing thoughts) to flourish and reap the benefits of a vase full of cut flowers (more positive, growth thoughts), we have to choke out the weeds (negative, hurtful, blame, self-limiting belief thoughts).

How does one do this? By taking on the role of master gardener of your mind. Weed out the negative thoughts right now by *consciously* sowing positive thoughts. When you plant constructive, peaceful, goal-related thoughts in the conscious part of your mind, your highly sensitive subconscious mind will be at work behind the scenes 24 hours a day to find ways to bring them to fruition. Yes, that's right – 24 hours a day.

If you choose, you can also reap the benefits of your subconscious mind while you sleep. At night as you settle down to go to sleep, give your subconscious mind homework. Let me give you a personal example. Using my conscious mind, I consider what I'd like my subconscious mind to support. For instance, as I write this book, I focus on my desire to help women. I visualize an opportunity to be recognized by Oprah and have her recommend my book through her book club. I visualize my book cover in one of her web blasts as a recommendation, and feel the pride of accomplishment and happiness that so many women will be exposed to this valuable guide.

I concentrate on the continued creative support and the motivation to stay focused. I see myself smiling and happy at book signing events, as I hear the success stories of women who have changed their lives in a positive way by taking action after reading my book.

While we sleep, our subconscious mind is busy looking for ways to support and solve our desires.

 You might as well give it something positive and creative to do, as it's working all night anyhow!

 A whole life transformation will result from a better understanding of the interactions and functions of your conscious and subconscious mind.

The Power of Our Thoughts

In his book *Quantum Healing*, Dr. Deepak Chopra cited a research study that concluded the average person thinks approximately 65,000 thoughts per day. Russ Harris, in his book *The Happiness Trap*, estimates that 80% of everyone's thoughts contain some sort of **negative** content. Moreover, it was reported that close to 95% *of our daily thoughts* are recycled from the previous day. This means we keep reinforcing negative ideas, day after day, in our minds.

So you can understand how negative thoughts can be draining. That's why it is important to learn to be mindful of these disempowering and negative thoughts. Then, as they enter our conscious mind, make a concerted effort to turn them around or, at the very least, neutralize them.

There are many things in life over which we have no control; yet we will always have some control over our thoughts. Thoughts become beliefs and those beliefs feed our mindset. Our actions are then governed by that mindset. In a nutshell, if your mindset is limiting your true potential, you will likely accept limited results in your life. Depending on what you believe possible, you may or may not perform certain actions, which then lead to specific results. For instance, I want to be a writer. If I did not believe I could write a book, there is a good chance I would not be sitting at my computer today typing this manuscript.

Self-Limiting Beliefs

According to Morty Lefkoe, creator of the Lefkoe Belief Process, "a belief is a statement about reality that we think is *the* truth.[21]" It is usually formed from a number of similar experiences we have had throughout our lives. Much of our belief system is learned thought patterns we have carried forward based on messages received in early childhood, even before the age of six. Some of these messages were informative, nurturing, positive, and helpful to our growth; others were toxic and self-limiting untruths, which now hold us hostage. These messages are instilled through feedback from parents and other authority figures, and general messages from society, all of which are in our sphere of influence from a young age. Parents and others did not intend for this to happen; they did the best they could and simply did not comprehend the effects their words and behaviors would have on our young minds. Throughout our lives we continue to build on those early messages and, cumulatively, they represent a lifetime of beliefs.

These limiting beliefs are represented by unconscious mental blocks, excuses, justifications, negative patterns, and routines, mental habits repeating themselves, and fears or other obstacles that stand in the way of us living our optimal lives in the present. They represent the past, old stories and ways of being. These beliefs easily trick us into thinking we are not fully capable of something, which causes us to question things like our worthiness, our power, and our competence. Our responses to these questions greatly influence what we do and don't act upon in life and can greatly affect our overall happiness. To heal and awaken the Goddess within – the goal of section one of this

---

[21] http://www.mortylefkoe.com/020910/

book – requires some work on these perceived limitations as a vital part of the transformation process.

Eliminating a Limiting Belief

If you were to empty out that little black bag that holds all your beliefs and evaluate each one under the light of consciousness, you would find some of them are no longer relevant and some have no basis in reality. You would find that some are disempowering, preventing you from attaining the results you desire; some need a validity recheck and others need to be replaced entirely.

Realizing a particular belief has a negative impact on the results you want in life is key to creating the life you truly want. Our limiting beliefs are a problem, because we have believed them so long that we have developed a deep-rooted emotional attachment to them. We begin to believe they are not just beliefs, but THE TRUTH. This makes them hard to find, as they live in the subconscious and often unquestioned part of our mind, deeply interwoven with our perceptions.

You may have heard the famous Henry Ford quote, "Whether you believe you can, or you believe you can't, you're right." Bearing this in mind, it is worth the effort to plant positive thoughts, beliefs, and attitudes in our mind garden and provide them with the sunlight they need to bloom bountifully and enrich all the possible results life will bring our way.

 ## Exercise: Identifying Limiting Beliefs

Take a moment to answer the following questions.

1. What rules have I created in my life that could be limiting my ability to pursue my goals and dreams?

   _____

   _____

_____

_____

2. What negative thoughts reoccur in my head every time I think about pursuing my goals and dreams? Which disempower my good intentions of getting started?

    _____

    _____

    _____

    _____

3. What incorrect assumptions do I make about committing to these goals and dreams?

    _____

    _____

    _____

    _____

4. What stereotypical beliefs am I allowing to hinder me from pursuing my goals and dreams?

    _____

    _____

    _____

    _____

5. What self-defeating meanings have I created based on my past failures with important goals? How do these meanings limit me and become barriers to goal-setting?

    _____

    _____

    _____

    _____

Self-Reflection Exercise – My Transformation Begins!

Complete the statements below as honestly and comprehensively as you can. Remember that for sustainable change, the motivation has to come from within. Dig deep and document everything you can think of, no matter how trivial it may seem. If it comes to mind, it must have some importance in the larger scheme of things. Your responses will provide you with guidance on where you need to focus your energy in your transformational journey.

Using your positive growth mindset, write down your beliefs about yourself, your strengths, and what you deserve in life. Use the following leads to guide your reflection. Document anything positive that comes to mind.

I am …

_____

_____

_____

I always …

_____

_____

_____

I want …

_____

_____

_____

I am capable of …

_____

_____

_____

I deserve …

_____

_____

_____

Which of these words would you use to describe yourself? Choose all that apply.

Inventive	☐	Thoughtful	☐	Cheerful	☐	Adventurous	☐
Practical	☐	Proactive	☐	Productive	☐	Positive	☐
Balanced	☐	Patient	☐	Enthusiastic	☐	Independent	☐
Original	☐	Generous	☐	Consistent	☐	Devoted	☐
Logical	☐	Outgoing	☐	Cooperative	☐	Professional	☐
Ethical	☐	Honest	☐	Motivated	☐	Trustworthy	☐
Mature	☐	Friendly	☐	Resourceful	☐	Focused	☐
Unique	☐	Confident	☐	Respectful	☐	Kind/Caring	☐
Tactful	☐	Intuitive	☐	Funny	☐	Perceptive	☐
Curious	☐	Pleasant	☐	Flexible	☐	Helpful	☐

Identify others, not listed, that positively describe you.

_____	☐	_____	☐	_____	☐	_____	☐
_____	☐	_____	☐	_____	☐	_____	☐
_____	☐	_____	☐	_____	☐	_____	☐
_____	☐	_____	☐	_____	☐	_____	☐

Which of these descriptors are you most proud of and why?

_____

_____

_____

What is the most empowering thing you could believe about yourself?

_____

_____

_____

_____

_____

With this empowering belief as your focus, what areas of your life do you want to transform?

_____

_____

_____

_____

_____

Who can you call upon as a supporter in your transformation?

_____

_____

_____

_____

_____

When you are successful in taking some positive steps in the right direction, how do you plan to reward yourself?

_____

_____

_____

_____

_____

 Positive Affirmations Related to Our Thoughts and Mindset:

- My positive mindset attracts success in my life.
- I choose a growth mindset; I am in charge of my emotions and my thoughts.

- I can do anything I choose to do, as my mindset is focused on personal growth.
- I can create the life I deserve with my thoughts, beliefs, and mindset.
- I am the source of my power. My thoughts, beliefs, and mindset are my power.

Chapter 7

Ending the Blame Game

"It makes one a better person to have had hardships and to have overcome hardships and not to blame anybody else for your mistakes." *Maureen Forrester*

Goddess Tenet #5: A Goddess is gentle and firm in communicating her boundaries, and protects herself from violation of them.

Goddess Leslie, age 68 from Massachusetts, United States shares her story:

I am counting the days until my handsome, hardworking husband will join me in retirement. It's September 2006.

I am visualizing morning coffee on the patio, trips to Hawaii to see our daughter, and stress-free dinners with friends ... but most of all, my heart yearns to spend simple, uninterrupted time with my high school sweetheart, enjoying all the luxuries of life. Retirement day is here. I am so grateful and excited to start our new adventure. The Golden Years have arrived!

Weeks pass and there is no mention of "together time," trips to Hawaii, or stress-free dinners with friends. I am becoming uneasy. When I flip the calendar to November and realize I am still playing the waiting game, I try to rationalize my uneasy feelings by blaming myself for not giving my husband enough time to adjust to his new unscheduled life.

I remain silent.

By the time I start decorating for Christmas, I realize my silence has been interpreted as "all is well" and we have settled into a comfortable pattern, on separate paths. I blame myself for having such high expectations, and decide to be grateful for what I have and give the "Golden Years Retirement Dream" more time to evolve. Taking the blame makes it easier to cope with my disappointment.

The New Year arrives and my personal dream of Retirement Bliss is still dormant. I suddenly realize blaming myself for unfulfilled dreams is taking its toll. I feel sad and defeated. I cry more and am falling into self-pity and depression.

My yoga class resumes in February and I am delighted to be reunited with my friends. I put on my happy face, exchange holiday stories, and unroll my yoga mat. One of my closest friends, who traveled over the holidays, taps me on the shoulder and asks, "What's going on behind those happy eyes? What's wrong? What are you hiding?" I begin to tear up, so we decide to continue the conversation after class. My silence needs to be broken. I need to reach out, face the truth, and stop hiding behind a cloud of self-blame.

A change is brewing.

An hour passes as I open my heart and let the flood of emotion and disappointment over my vision of The Golden Years spill out between sobs and tears.

I am blessed to have my monologue fall on understanding ears. Another hour passes as my wise woman friend explains how we all can get caught in the web of self-blame, especially women, who by nature are *nurturers and want to keep all things in perfect order. Her suggestions to improve my situation are simple.*

I return home, reflect on our heart-to-heart conversation, and make a list of changes I need to implement in my life ...

1. *Be kind to myself. Be my own best friend.*
2. *Know others' life choices have nothing to do with me.*
3. *Live* **my** *best life. Invite those I love to join me – like my spouse.*
4. *Plan trips to Hawaii to see my daughter and ask my spouse to join me.*
5. *Expand my Reiki practice. Use my gifts.*

I decide to look up the definition of self-blame on the Internet. I find it a bit frightening.

Michael Formica, who has been a practicing clinician for 25 years, states in one of his blogs, "Self-blame is one of the most toxic forms of emotional abuse. It amplifies our perceived inadequacies, whether real or imagined, and paralyzes us before we can even begin to move forward."

As I read the article[22] my eyes grow bigger – I have been caught in the web. Perusing the page, my eyes fall on the following quote:

> **You, yourself, as much as anyone else in the entire Universe, deserve your love and affection. ~The Buddha**

This quote resonates with me ... it makes so much sense! Instantly, I decide to make a conscious effort to banish self-blame from my thoughts and, to quote Oprah, start "living my best life." A weight is lifted from my shoulders. I feel liberated.

It takes several months for the transition to Blameless Me to take place. Changing a mindset can be very difficult, and it is easy to slip,

---

[22] https://www.psychologytoday.com/blog/enlightened-living/201304/self-blame-the-ultimate-emotional-abuse

but now I am aware of the "web of blame" and I can make an easy shift in thoughts, when needed.

Since then, I have taken several trips to see my daughter, some solo and some with my spouse, but all have been a joy. I no longer feel I am to blame when others do not see my "vision."

My joyful heart has returned.

And, my biggest achievement, I have expanded my Reiki business. Because I was willing to make some "uncomfortable" changes in my lifestyle, mainly banishing self-blame, I can honestly say, **life is good.**

* * *

As Goddess Leslie's story demonstrates, the blame game keeps many of us stuck. We keep ourselves trapped when we blame others for our life circumstances. The trap is even deeper when we blame *ourselves* for everything. Knowing that our outer world is merely a reflection of our inner world may inspire us to try to reconcile who is to blame for the issues that have taken and continue to take place in our lives. Taking responsibility doesn't mean blaming ourselves; it simply means we have the ability to make new responses.

Blaming Others

> "You take your life in your own hands, and what happens? A terrible thing; no one to blame."
> *Erica Jong*

To blame as a verb is defined in the Merriam Webster dictionary as, "To say or think that a person or thing is responsible for something bad that has happened."[23]

Why is it so common to blame others? Is it because we feel the things that are happening to us are outside our control and others

---

[23] http://www.merriam-webster.com/dictionary/blame

are to blame? Are our poor financial situations, job dissatisfaction, or tattered relationship woes someone *else's* fault?

Blaming others will not make our problems go away; it only adds to them. Blame is about avoiding responsibility and not addressing the real issues. We are adults now; *awakening Goddesses, in fact!* We know we have made mistakes in our lives, just as others have made mistakes that have affected us. Placing blame puts us in the helpless victim category and leaves us powerless to make positive, lasting changes in our lives.

When you release the blame, you can get on with living your life! By beginning to step onto the spiritual path, choosing positive thoughts and having the right mindset, you have already taken a step away from blaming behavior.

I believe we are here on Earth to learn lessons. If we can treat mistakes as an opportunity to learn, we will greatly reduce the blame contagion and the finger-pointing habit that runs rampant in our society. But if we fail to learn from our mistakes and keep repeating them, the lessons will continue. We need to learn the lessons before we can move forward.

There is great value in reflecting on the consequences of the choices we have made, as well as those made for us.

You may find this section difficult because it dredges up parts of your life you are trying to avoid. Be completely honest and address whatever you are trying to avoid, because this is more than likely the root of your *stuckness*. You might have to admit that you contributed to a situation for which you are blaming others, and start to take responsibility for your choices and actions.

 We cannot be passive participants in life. We are at a major intersection in life, and we have to step up to the plate and confront our situation in order to change where we are at …

 … which I would remind you is … restless and stuck!

Some women blame their parents for their relationship difficulties, claiming they were not good relationship role models. Perhaps you were raised with cold critical parents who didn't know how to love, so you never learned how to express this emotion. Perhaps you blame your parents for their indifference, which led you to develop these same negative behaviors now contributing to your life problems. You may blame a past or current life partner for contributing to your current situation of *stuckness* because of something that person did or didn't say or do, to or for you. You may blame a child for the strain and drain their actions have caused or continue to cause, disabling you from fully living your life. This is just a small sample of possible blame factors. The opportunity to assign blame to others is ample, if this is your propensity.

This is a problem that possibly affects more than 25% of the US population, according to Bill Eddy, author of the book *It's All Your Fault!: 12 Tips for Managing People Who Blame Others for Everything*. We seem to have evolved into a pervasive blame culture. We put more emphasis on transferring blame and letting ourselves off the hook than resolving situations; it seems passing blame to another is easier than delving into the root of the problem.

Blaming others interferes with our ability to think about how we can move forward and what we could do to make life better. In other words, finding and dwelling on blame becomes the bigger focus and thus more important than fixing the situation. However, we imagine we have solved the problem, by passing that blame onto others.

If you have fallen into the trap of blaming others for your own painful reactions, you might now be reflecting that this course of action has not served you well, and has likely damaged or even ruined some of your precious relationships. It takes a lot of courage to admit – inwardly and then outwardly – that you made mistakes and the responsibility for various problems in your life does not fall solely on another person.

Instead of looking at the situation from a subjective personal view, try to view it from the objective view of another – let's say from the perspective of the person you are blaming. Why did they act the way they did? Why did they do what they did? Is there a new way to view what happened and the resulting fallout? Remember growth is about learning. Any time we let go of our attachment to a problem and stop blaming another person, we create a learning opportunity and pave the way for freedom and a brighter future for ourselves.

Blaming Ourselves

Blame can rear its ugly head and invade our lives in a variety of ways. Some of the most common focuses of my blame have been: my past, my family, my body image, my job, situations that occur in the world that just don't make sense, balancing my multiple responsibilities, my schedule, and others. I have blamed myself for making mistakes, for procrastination, for over-reacting, for my lack of effective time management skills, for forgetting to save my computer files often enough and losing valuable work. Internally, I was once a master at the self-blame game. I was my worst enemy, at times. I am not unique, though; this is a common theme among women. It is something I had to work hard at overcoming.

Research shows that women are more prone to blaming themselves. Interestingly, men tend to project blame onto others.[24]

 Careful you don't get caught as the filling in a blame sandwich!

I am sure we would all agree that we admire people who step up to the plate and take responsibility for something that is their fault. Too much blame does not a happy life make!

 It's time to stop the *"should-ing"* on yourself. Ban the toxic word *should* from your vocabulary.

---

[24] Dattner, B. (2011). *The Blame Game: How the hidden rules of credit and blame determine our success or failure.* Free Press

When we blame ourselves for a bad decision, we inflict damage to one of the most important attributes we possess – our sense of self-esteem. We need to work on building up our self-esteem and showing ourselves self-compassion. We need to walk a fine line between over-externalizing and blaming others and over-internalizing and blaming ourselves when problems occur. Doing too much of either puts us out of balance and makes us unhappy. In either scenario, the resulting blame is cruel and destructive to our lives. It sets up a situation that burdens us with shame and guilt.

 This burden hinders our ability to move forward and closer to the goal of "The Happy Goddess" who lives her life with purpose and passion. Reaching this goal means we need to see the wisdom of taking our life into our own Goddess hands and molding it into what we truly desire.

For many years now, when something has gone wrong in my world, I have tried to shift my mindset to going hard on the problem and soft on the people involved, including myself. This paradigm shift has allowed me to reduce self-blame and help others look for solutions – not focusing so much on blaming people, thereby reducing their own blame of others.

Self-Reflection Exercise: Ending the Blame Game

The following reflective questions are designed to raise awareness of how you assign blame. Awareness is always the starting point to realizing there is a need to change.

1. Looking back on situations that have gone wrong in your life, do you acknowledge and accept your part in the less-than-ideal results or focus on finger pointing? Write about

a situation and your response(s) from a blame-assignment perspective here.

_____

_____

_____

_____

_____

2. When things go wrong, is your propensity primarily to blame yourself or to blame others?

_____

_____

_____

_____

_____

3. Do you suffer from the "should have and should not have" syndrome where your mind focuses on and regurgitates self-blame over and over again?

_____

_____

_____

_____

_____

4. When things go wrong, do you tend to put more energy into problem solving or blame assignment?

_____

_____

_____

_____

_____

5. Do you take responsibility for things that are not yours to own (e.g. the imperfections of life, other people's feelings and experiences)?

_____

_____

_____

_____

Life brings many challenges and getting past the big ones, the ones over which we have no control, requires a period of grieving. Over time, grieving brings acceptance. This acceptance builds in us the fortitude to minimize the habit of blaming ourselves and others. It is time to stop playing the blame game. Games are supposed to be fun; if they're not fun, who wants to play them?

In order to take responsibility for how we wish to be treated, we need to take responsibility for ourselves, and let everyone else do the same. How do we do this, you ask? Whether they have asked for it or not, we need to consider who we need to forgive so that we can free ourselves to create this amazing life we want and deserve. The next chapter on forgiveness will assist you with this challenging, yet rewarding, task.

 ## Positive Affirmations Related to Blame:

- I release the blame from each and every struggle I face.
- I choose acceptance and compassion toward all humanity.
- Today, I will be gentle with myself.
- I take responsibility for my actions.
- The past is just that; I live only in the present.

Chapter 8

Compassionate Forgiveness

"When you hold resentment toward another, you are bound to that person or condition by an emotional link that is stronger than steel. Forgiveness is the only way to dissolve that link and get free."
Catherine Ponder

Goddess Tenet #7: A Goddess is committed to peace and harmony, and does her part in healing the earth, as a fundamental principle of her being.

Goddess Andrea, age 52, from Quebec, Canada tells her story:

A steel cage surrounded my head, bolted to the top of my skull. Two bags of clear fluid and one bag of blood flowed into my body. The machine beside me, which made a suctioning noise, was attached to my throat. A beeping noise replicated my heartbeat. I faded in and out each time, seeing different faces. They were speaking to me, but I could not hear them. An obese man laughed at me from a panel on the ceiling of my room. Sometimes I would see a rat on my chest looking down at me, or large spiders hanging from the ceiling or on the walls. It seemed like every hour someone was pulling my body forward in the bed and inserting something hard behind me.

Three months later, the morphine dosage was decreased and the reality of many things came to light. I realized the man on the ceiling, the rats, the spiders were all hallucinations caused by the medication. I also realized that every morning at 6 am an x-ray machine was inserted behind me in my bed. I felt as though it was happening every hour, but in reality it was every 24 hours.

I felt like I had been run over by a transport truck. I was out of the trauma unit before I could start to understand what had happened to me. I had been run over by a transport truck. All but the back two feet of my car had been under it, with me inside.

I was now a C5/6 quadriplegic, paralyzed from the chest down due to this life-changing accident. I understood that I would never walk again, but I did not realize there was so much more to my injury than just not being able to walk. I learned I had also suffered two heart attacks in the first two weeks of hospitalization.

As I began to be able to think more clearly, my first thought was of my boys. I had left them with a sitter and never returned. I had not seen them for three months and now they were coming to visit me. I had a big smile on my face, waiting for them to enter the room. My eight-year-old entered with his head down. When he looked up, we both burst into tears. He looked at me like he'd never seen me before; he appeared to be afraid of me. I did not realize that over the three months I had lost approximately 40 pounds. My hair had fallen out and the sparse amount that had grown back was dark and curly. My cheeks were sunken and I looked like I was 70 years old. My six-year-old son stayed in the parking lot, too afraid to come see me.

I quickly realized I needed to fight and be strong for the sake of my boys. A light had come on and my mindset shifted to one of thinking positively. I had to do whatever it took to get home and have my children with me. Every time I looked at my surroundings, I would set a goal, conquer that goal, and move on to the next. One of my first goals was to be discharged from the trauma hospital where I had spent six months, and be admitted to a rehabilitation center, where I would spend the next five months.

The rehabilitation facility I was sent to is one where people with catastrophic injuries are taught to live with a disability. I learned all about my injury and what to expect with regard to how the body functions due to paralysis. I also learned about software and assisted devices to improve my quality of living.

I realized I was lucky to be alive, and that a completely different roadmap would need to be planned out for me. Returning home to live with my boys was my focus. I sold my home and purchased a new home through pictures, while living in the rehab hospital. I was discharged Friday, July 21, 2001. I headed home by taxi to be greeted by a personal support worker, hired to assist me with daily living. After almost a year in hospital, it felt strange being in a new home that I had never seen before, with unfamiliar and very sparse furnishings. All my clothes were hanging neatly in the closet, but none of them fit me. There was a manual Hoyer lift in the corner that was used to get me in and out of bed. There was so much to accomplish, and everything had to be done one slow step at a time.

Child and youth workers were with my boys seven days a week, once I was discharged. The workers' objective was to make the boys' transition back into the home with me as smooth as possible. They were both sent to anger management sessions with a child psychologist during this process. After just over two years, my boys moved back to start the school year in September 2002. We continued to have child and youth workers visit us four to five days per week for another year.

Eighteen months after my injury, I attended a mediation with my personal injury lawyer. There were several people present representing the trucking company, while my lawyer told the heart-wrenching details of my life as a quadriplegic.

"Andrea was an independent single mom working at a hospital, raising two small boys, at the time of her injury," she explained. She then detailed how the accident had left me paralyzed from the chest down, unable to live a normal life. "Andrea can no longer use her bladder or bowel function without assistance. She cannot use any of her limbs, nor does she have any sensation below the chest. She is confined to an electric wheelchair or a bed, which comes with many more health issues, such as muscle atrophy, muscle spasms, loss of sensation – including the ability to feel heat or cold – bone density depletion and skin sores." She explained the changes I was facing related to sexual function, sexual sensitivity, and fertility caused by damage to the nerve fibers in my spinal cord. System by system, she outlined the new realities I was facing and ended with the fact that I required 24-hour caregiver assistance in order to function with daily living.

When the mediation was over, I noted several of the parties had tears in their eyes. Leaving, I wheeled down a long hallway and noticed that many rooms had large tables with chairs all around – meeting rooms, I assumed. I noticed a room on the left side with the door closed. I stopped to look inside, as the door had a small window. I saw a man sitting in the room with his head down. He looked very pale and nervous. My lawyer briskly directed me to move along, and at that moment I realized this was the man driving the transport the day I was injured. He looked up, hearing the noise in the hallway, and saw me staring at him. The man looked so sad, distraught, and in his eyes I could see and feel the sorrow he was speaking to me. I felt a wave of empathy, and the anger that was inside me started to release. I left the mediation feeling a little better. I realized I had started to release blame and to forgive, that day. Over the next few weeks, daily life seemed a little easier. I had started to transform mentally based on that forgiveness, and that allowed me to move forward ... and move forward I have!

I have taken six or seven courses through online learning. I learned various Microsoft software applications. I took creative writing and I completed a web design course, all without the use of my hands. Two years after the accident and despite very poor circulation due to my injuries, and therefore always feeling cold, I attended as many of my son's hockey games as I could.

Six years after I returned home, I became a peer support volunteer for a National spinal injury association. I have been called upon 12 or more times by the same rehabilitation hospital I attended and have traveled back there to help other people who have suffered a catastrophic injury integrate back into the community. They ask me about all sorts of things, from mobility devices to relationships and clothing, and I provide them with information and inspiration. I have also sent my staff to the home of two teenaged girls – sisters who became quadriplegics in the same accident – to train their personal support workers in how to meet their needs.

I now have a staff of personal support workers with me 24 hours a day to assist me with intermittent catheterization to empty my bladder and any other matters I need help with, not having the use of my limbs.

I challenge myself with home renovation projects. I buy properties that need repairs, hire a contractor, and oversee those renovations. Keeping busy with these projects keeps my mind active, which leaves no time for negative thoughts.

It was a long haul, but with determination, consistency, and persistence, our lives are now as normal as that of any other family. I am grateful to be living, and I feel I might as well live the best I can.

* * *

This story demonstrates that forgiveness can bring about the kind of peace that helps us move on with our lives. Forgiveness is a virtue essential to recovery. Despite what some believe, forgiveness is not a sign of weakness but a mark of strength. It does not mean we justify or condone the situation or wrongful act; hurtful actions have consequences. It does not mean we remove the other person's responsibility for hurting us, or that we have to reconcile with them. Forgiveness is recognizing that what has happened has happened; and that because it is in the past, there is no way to undo it and hence no reason to let the situation influence and dictate the rest of our life.

The best way to increase your own physical and mental health is to find the compassion to forgive others; not simply for their sake, but for your own.

The problems we face related to holding onto past hurts are vast. As we experience shame, negativity, bitterness, and anger, we head straight toward low self-esteem, low self-confidence, low self-respect, and self-sabotage. There is no grey area when it comes to forgiveness. Forgiveness is a choice. You choose to forgive or you choose to continue to live with the resulting anger, bitterness, resentment, blame, grudge-holding, and host of other negative emotions. The ability to forgive allows you to shed the excess baggage of negativity that dwelling on hurtful situations or events can add to your life. These negative feelings and behaviors do not support finding a logical, solution-oriented mindset in the face of life's challenges.

Do you want to be a woman who operates at a lower frequency, focusing on revenge and experiencing the anger and hatred that go along with it? Or would you rather be a Goddess who operates at the higher frequency of forgiveness; someone filled with empathy, love, and compassion? Forgiveness is a compassionate gift you give yourself. The transformative process forgiveness brings about will result in improvements to your life: healthier lifestyles, positive energy, better relationships, lowered stress, and potential increases in both longevity and prosperity.

 I encourage you to put on your rose-colored *forgiveness* glasses and try to look at the person separate from the offense. Are they a person who generally cares for others? What are their good characteristics? My experience is that this thought process will induce a paradigm shift.

I'd like to share my story about someone I hadn't realized I needed to forgive:

A number of years ago, I found a website where you could enter the name of the person you wanted to forgive, the reason for the forgiveness, and then your own name. I entered my father's name, and said I forgave him for taking his own life when the family needed him so much. I then added my own name. This symbolic gesture gave me some closure to feelings that were not conducive to my best interests.

At the time of his death, I was the second oldest of five siblings. Our dad had not lived with us for a few years. While he was a good man who loved all five of his children, he was also an alcoholic and suffered from depression. He wrote me a poem for my 13th birthday, in a little autograph book I had gotten that same day as a birthday gift. I cherished that poem and kept it for those seven years between receiving it and his death. When he died, I placed the original in his casket, but I know that poem by heart.

A father's wish should be unique, and tell a simple story.
This wish is a little weak, with not a lot of glory:
I hope your life will always be as happy as you've been to me;
And as you go through passing fads, always remember you have a Dad.

I needed to forgive him for not living up to that promise. He wasn't there to walk me down the aisle at my wedding or even meet the man I chose to marry. He wasn't there to welcome any of my three wonderful sons into the world or watch them grow into the fine men they are today. He wasn't there to watch over my brother, his only son, and prevent him from driving drunk the night he died in a car accident, leaving his own teenage son and daughter without a dad, thereby repeating history.

My dad had been dead for over 30 years, but I realized in that moment that I needed to forgive him; not for his sake, but for my own. Having said that, the newly awakened, spiritually-infused me feels that he, too, had been suffering all that time because of my lack of forgiveness, and that he had been there watching over me during all those milestones in my life. Choosing to forgive my father has freed up all kinds of emotional space within me. I no longer carry around resentment or anger about the past, and thus am more fully involved with the present.

***

A teacher wanted to present a lesson of forgiveness to her students in a non-traditional way. She asked them each to bring a backpack to class. She in turn brought a large bag of rocks and asked the students to write the name of each person they refused to forgive on a rock and place the rocks in their backpack. She then asked the students to place the backpack on their backs and keep it there at all times. The hassle and weight of physically lugging this heavy backpack made it clear to the students what the teacher was trying to convey about the burden of non-forgiveness, and the physical and spiritual pain of carrying around such a heavy load through life.

I heard this story in the distant past, but never forgot the lesson it provides on the price we pay for holding onto our pain. Forgiveness is a life decision we make to release an event so that it no longer has power over us.

 Give yourself the gift of forgiveness and take back your power!

 Forgiveness Exercise

Clinical psychologist Dr. Everett Worthington, an expert on forgiveness and a professor of psychology, has developed a five-step process for forgiveness, which he calls REACH.[25] The following forgiveness exercise outlines his model and incorporates some reflective learning questions for your response. Although I have left space for you to document here, you may wish to use your journal to reflect on these questions, to explore your thoughts in greater detail.

---

[25] http://www.evworthington-forgiveness.com/research/

Step 1: Recall

Think of an event (or events) in your life that may require your forgiveness. Recall the event(s) as impartially and in as much factual detail as you can. Outline in detail the when, what, and who of the event. Detail your feelings of the situation, both when the event occurred and now.

_____

_____

_____

_____

_____

Step 2: Empathize

Take a step back and make an effort to understand what occurred from the point of view of the person(s) who wronged you. Put yourself in the other person's shoes and look at the situation from their perspective. Did you have a bit of a paradigm shift from this reflection?

_____

_____

_____

_____

_____

Step 3: Altruistic Gift of Forgiveness

Think back to a time when you wronged someone and were forgiven by him or her. Now, offer this gift to the person who wronged you. Document who has forgiven you in the past, and for what. Now reflect on that situation and consider what it meant for them and what it meant for you.

_____

_____

_____

_____

_____

Step 4: Commit

Commit yourself (or others) to this forgiveness. You may write a letter of forgiveness to the person you forgive (which you do not have to mail); you may write about the situation and why you choose to forgive them in the space below, or in your journal. If it is appropriate and would not do more harm, you may choose to tell the person who wronged you that you forgive them.

_____

_____

_____

_____

_____

Step 5: Hold

Reminders of the wrong will bring back the negative, hurt feelings. Hold true to your personal choice of forgiveness as the gift you gave yourself. Below, I suggest you take this pledge, and then sign and date your notation.

I have chosen to forgive _____ for the wrong I felt was done against me. I know that future situations will remind me of this matter, but I have given myself the gift of forgiveness and as these negative thoughts arise, I will remember this pledge and that I forgave _____ not for their sake, but for my own happiness.

On this_____ (date), I _____ hereby confirm to hold my forgiveness pledge from this day forward.

According to happiness expert and author Marci Shimoff, "When you forgive, you heal your own anger and hurt and are able to **let love lead again**. It's like spring cleaning for your heart."

 ## Positive Affirmations Related to Forgiveness:

- I accept that I did the best I could with what I knew at the time.
- I have the courage to forgive and become whole again.
- I free myself from the heavy weight of anger, resentment, guilt, and shame.
- I release the past so I can step into the present with pure intentions.

Section II

Nurturing and Loving
the Goddess Within

Chapter 9

Boosting Self-Confidence

"Optimism is the faith that leads to achievement. Nothing can be done without hope and confidence." *Helen Keller*

Goddess Tenet #9: A Goddess lives her life authentically, portraying the same façade to the external world as she holds close to her heart.

Goddess Lily, age 57, from Morocco, North Africa tells her story:

Have you ever felt like you're not good enough? That you don't deserve the money and success other people have? If so, you're far from alone. We all feel this way at some point in our lives.

We are not born with these thoughts already installed in our brain. Someone planted these seeds during our childhood, or perhaps when we were in the midst of a bad relationship. If we believe there's even a grain of truth to the remarks that we hear, we internalize these thoughts; and over time they become beliefs, which in turn become our reality. It's a bit like downloading a computer virus. We don't know that it has happened until we go to use a program and find that the virus had corrupted it. *If our program called "Life" isn't working as well as it should, it might be riddled with thought viruses.*

I recently had an encounter with a thought virus I was sure had been deleted from the hard drive of my mind. I was adopted by my parents when I was very young, and I was dating a guy who had issues with adoptees. His first wife had been born with fetal alcohol syndrome, adopted, and later became an alcoholic. As a result, he believed all adoptees must be flawed in some way.

I am a professional life coach and have undergone extensive training in letting go of limiting beliefs. Even so, this guy really pushed my buttons. I was immediately overcome by shame, remembering my mother telling me as a child that I might have bad blood because she didn't know where I had come from. As I opened my mouth to defend myself against my boyfriend's remarks, I realized what I was doing. I was giving away my power and going back to that girl who had to please everyone, achieve high marks, and get the promotions to prove to the world that she wasn't a potential axe murderer. Essentially, I was trying to justify my existence.

Who would I have been if I had run with my mother's story? Someone afraid to have kids in case they turned out "bad." A woman scared of success in case anyone saw through my professional veneer to my potentially evil core. As it happens, I have a strong sense of justice and an inquiring mind, and my mother's story of my "bad blood" just didn't stand up. It was never true; it was just a construct of my mother's own fears. The true story is that I'm a successful self-made woman with two beautiful adult children. My mission is to energize, empower, and elevate other women, so they can speak and live their truth with joy.

The lesson I learned is not to hide my light under a bushel. We are not better or worse than anyone else; we are ourselves, with our own passions and talents. Beware of people wanting to put you into a small box and limit you with a label of their own creation, born from a place of fear. Don't let someone else's version of your story hold you back from living the life you want. You are amazing, you matter, and you are enough!

* * *

To be successful in life and achieve our goals, it is crucial that we possess self-confidence. Self-confidence, defined here as "having assurance in our own abilities," is a quality that changes our lives because it provides us with an absolute sense of control over our destinies. For many of us stuck Goddesses, this is sadly lacking or may even be a foreign concept. Imagine living a life *not* plagued with doubts and fears related to your capabilities, but instead believing you can achieve anything you set your mind to. This doesn't have to be a pipe dream. Self-confidence can be learned.

Knowing the roots of self-confidence is a good place to start. When we are children, we begin to develop self-confidence whenever our accomplishments are recognized. If loving beings such as our parents or grandparents are present to cheer us on, this encouragement is confidence-promoting. Conversely, if a child grows up in a hostile and critical environment, where destructive criticism and a lack of love are the predominant influences, or where the child is conditioned to feel fear, rejection or indifference, any confidence they have built through their own internal mechanisms will be eroded.

As we continue into adolescence, our families, friends, and other significant individuals who make up our support system continue to have a major influence on our lives. We all have at least one story where someone close to us made a comment that took us down a few notches on the precious self-confidence measuring stick and affected us for several years after. Our level of confidence and self-assuredness growing up has a lot to do with whether this support system is positive or negative for us. Our support system also influences our developing confidence in other areas, such as our body image, how intelligent we think we are, and so on.

For example, when I was a young, budding Goddess, my grandfather cruelly commented – in front of a room full of people – "I see you have two mosquito bites under your shirt," in reference to my breasts that were just starting to develop. I was horrified. I was already anxiously conscious of the changes I was going through, and I certainly didn't want a room full of people focusing on me or my body! That moment was a real confidence-deflator. Looking back, I remember my aunt pulled me aside and whispered something inspiring and positive, thereby rebalancing my self-confidence equilibrium at least a little.

As we continue through life, there are constant opportunities to build or deflate our confidence: success in finding a soul mate, educational achievements, children, a career, breakups, getting downsized or fired, loss, and many others. Without the foundational framework to support us, the negative situations will only deflate our self-confidence.

The more time you spend consciously thinking about the person you want to be and the traits you wish to have, the more you cue your subconscious mind to come up with ways to make these desires a reality. Once again, the power of your thoughts can help you transform in this area.

 According to the Law of Attraction, what you think about, you bring about!

In Chapter 6, we also learned that we may choose either a fixed mindset or a growth mindset. Hopefully, you picked *growth*. Now is the time to put this choice into action and move from *scared to death* to *unstoppable*, or some reasonable facsimile.

We demonstrate self-confidence in all kinds of ways, all the time. One-on-one discussions with others, the way we dress, our posture, how well we express our knowledge on a topic, our ability to engage others, our ability to admit it when we are wrong, and our ability to set and achieve goals are but a few examples.

Although I didn't know it at the time, my mother taught me some life lessons that positively shaped my self-confidence, and I'd like to share some of them with you.

Tips for Boosting Self-Confidence – Lessons from Mom

1. **Ms. Dress Up** – Putting thought into how you dress goes a long way in improving your self-confidence. Have you ever noticed that when you look good, you feel a whole lot better? There's this whole positive, feminine, sexy, aura that comes over us when we put some effort into how we look. My mom always taught my sisters and me that quality was much better than quantity. She ingrained in us the fact that quality clothes last longer, stay in style longer, and result in less closet clutter. You don't have to have a large budget to attain this goal.

2. **Sit Up Straight** – My mom always told us to pretend we had a yardstick tucked into the back of our pants. Slouching was severely frowned upon at home. The mantra I grew up with was: "Shoulders back, sit up straight, keep your head up." Good posture tells a story about a person and supports a positive first impression. Make an effort to practice good posture today – you will feel more confident! Mindset, perhaps, but whatever works – right?

3. **Smile** – Think of what happens when you smile at another person. Do you almost always get a smile right back from them? How does that make you feel? A little more courageous to engage in conversation with them, perhaps? Or a little more confident to take the next step in approaching them?

Remember: building self-confidence is all part of our ongoing personal development. Learning about and celebrating our strengths, and finding ways to address or sometimes simply accept our weaknesses, will go a long way in boosting our self-confidence. Let's take a bit of time here to celebrate our strengths.

Exercise: Personality Traits – Self-Reflection

1. Using a pencil, go through the following list and check off all the traits you feel accurately describe you in some way.
2. Feel free to add any others not already on the list.
3. Now go back through the list again and put a ☺ beside the ones you are particularly proud of and a TV (for Transforming Venus) beside the ones where you feel there may be an opportunity for some future personal development.

___ Accurate	___ Dependent	___ Initiates
___ Aggressive	___ Diligent	___ Integrity
___ Ambitious	___ Diplomatic	___ Intimidating
___ Analytical	___ Direct	___ Introverted
___ Approachable	___ Disciplined	___ Intuitive
___ Articulate	___ Disorganized	___ Irresponsible
___ Assertive	___ Down to earth	___ Meticulous
___ Athletic	___ Easy-going	___ Open-minded
___ Authentic	___ Effective	___ Optimistic
___ Calm	___ Efficient	___ Organized
___ Careful	___ Empathetic	___ Original
___ Competitive	___ Energetic	___ Outgoing
___ Confident	___ Enthusiastic	___ Patient
___ Conforming	___ Extroverted	___ Perfectionist
___ Conscientious	___ Fair	___ People-pleaser
___ Considerate	___ Flexible	___ Persistent
___ Consistent	___ Forgiving	___ Persuasive
___ Co-operative	___ Friendly	___ Positive
___ Courageous	___ Generous	___ Practical
___ Creative	___ Goal-oriented	___ Precise
___ Curious	___ High achiever	___ Professional
___ Decisive	___ Honest	___ Punctual
___ Demanding	___ Humorous	___ Quality-
___ Dependable	___ Independent	focused

___ Quick learner	___ Responsible	___ Serious
___ Realistic	___ Responsive	___ Team-oriented
___ Reliable	___ Self-confident	___ Tenacious
___ Resourceful	___ Self-controlled	
___ Respectful	___ Self-reliant	

Well done! You now have a working list of areas where you shine (☺) which should definitely play a part in boosting your self-confidence and your self-esteem. You may also have a second list of areas where you want to focus some personal development energy to transform further (TV).

 ## Bonus "Smiling" Exercise

I challenge you to make a conscious effort to smile at everyone you meet for a full day. This is a feel-good experiment for you and everyone who crosses your path that day. As a positive by-product, you will experience a little bit of Goddess transformation on the self-confidence front.

 ## Positive Affirmations Related to Self-Confidence:

- I am friendly, outgoing, and confident.
- I am a success in all that I do.
- I focus on my strengths more than I focus on my weaknesses.
- I focus on my successes more than I focus on my failures.

Chapter 10

Building Self-Esteem

"Self-esteem comes from being able to define the world in your own terms and refusing to abide by the judgments of others." *Oprah Winfrey*

Goddess Tenet #2: A Goddess is an evolutionary being who recognizes her responsibility to continue to learn and grow, both intellectually and spiritually.

Goddess Vivian, age 45, from Sydney, Australia tells her story:

"Vivian, don't be silly! You are so employable!"

My friend Melissa will never understand how much those simple words meant to me. Looking back, I can barely understand how they could have seemed so enormous then, but I guess self-esteem can either make or break you. And now, with a rational mind and healthy self-esteem, I completely agree with her.

I was a qualified Engineer, received academic excellence awards, had moved up the corporate ladder from engineering to corporate development before leaving to have children, run a couple of hobby businesses on the side, and helped my then-husband build a thriving small business.

I had skills, know-how, competence, intelligence, high standards, creativity, problem-solving skills, management skills, analytical skills, a willingness to try new things, all my own teeth, and was always well presented. I was MORE than employable; I was an absolute catch for any employer!

Those words helped pull me out of a deep hole and encouraged me to show up to a job interview that ended up being the first of many steps leading to the amazing life I now live.

But back then, it was a very different story. I would get knots in my stomach as I entered the parking lot of my son's prestigious private school, feeling like all eyes were on me. I feared somebody might one day politely ask me to leave or "please park that very average-looking Honda somewhere else."

Of course, nobody said any such thing. Everybody was very lovely. In fact, I'm sure they had no idea how out of place I felt or how embarrassed I was by the fact that I was a financially struggling single mom who had left her marriage with nothing more than two young children under her arm and a career that had spent eight years gathering dust.

My ex-husband, angry at my decision, was determined to make me suffer the brunt of his pain. I took on all the angry words, the put-downs, and the allegations of being a bad mother, of destroying our family, of being an unworthy human being. It nearly crushed me.

But I don't blame him for lashing out. Had I taken care of myself along the way, my self-esteem would have safely protected me from his rage, like a shield. I was the one who had made a grave mistake. I had allowed my self-esteem to wither away while I worried about what others thought of me, how THEY perceived me, and how well I was playing the part of the "good" mother, wife, friend, and socialite.

My self-worth was completely wrapped up in the opinions of others, mostly that of my ex-husband, so I found myself in a most unfortunate situation. I had given away my power. How I felt about ME was outside of my control – or at least, that's the scenario I had managed to create. I didn't know who I really was anymore, so how could I possibly feel good about myself? I had been so busy being what I thought everybody else wanted me to be, looking for reassurance, affirmation, and acceptance. A silent nod of approval would let me know I was playing my part well. What a path of self-destruction I had created!

I had to set about rebuilding my self-esteem, one piece at a time. I started with baby steps, doing whatever I could from where I was – doing anything at all. Finances were highest on the priority list, but I'd lost touch with my career and my children were young. I started delivering home order catalogues. It was slow, arduous work. I spent hours pushing my son's stroller up and down streets, organizing and delivering orders. For my efforts, I was paid approximately $50 per week in commissions. But it was a start.

The company asked me to become an area manager. They could see I was efficient, organized, and motivated. I started earning $100-150 per week in commissions. It seemed I was climbing another corporate ladder! Well, not quite, but it gave me the confidence to show up to the sales rep interview and get that good old-fashioned pep talk from my friend.

I got the job and met wonderful successful people who respected me. I did well. I continued to tell myself I was worthy, that I was smart and could do anything. I practiced affirmations, visualizations, anything to flood my subconscious mind with the news that I was back in business. I madly and outrageously celebrated every single step, no matter how trivial it seemed. I knew I was a wonderful, dedicated mother. I always managed to work around my children's school and pre-school hours – they never went into daycare, which was important to me.

I was asked to join a client's business, but my employer wanted me to stay. I'd done great work. I was an asset. I went ahead and joined *the other business. It didn't work out. I went backwards financially and wasted six months. Or did I? My self-esteem had grown stronger. I had been strengthening it like a muscle and it was now there to support me as I took a leap of faith and started my own business. Three years later, I was awarded a major national award and able to offer a friend a salary to support me in my business.*

I continued to celebrate, to acknowledge my wins at each little step along the way, both to stretch and to back myself. I ventured into new things. I wrote a book. It became a bestseller! I started speaking and coaching, helping others unscramble overwhelm and regain their clarity and focus. And this is where I find myself today.

The future is certain to bring amazing things I've not yet dared dream of, but I know my self-esteem is the fuel that will continue to propel me deeper and deeper into the adventures of time and space.

Remember that your self-esteem is like a muscle. Keep it healthy and nourish it, but also know that you can rebuild it when necessary. It will help you achieve incredible things.

Be kind to yourself in the process, practice patience, and take baby steps, doing what you can, from where you are. You truly do not have to see the whole staircase. Just take that first step.

See you up there.

* * *

There is often confusion between the definition of self-confidence and self-esteem. They are closely linked. One builds on the other; so the more self-confidence you possess, the higher your self-esteem will be. Similarly, the more you appreciate yourself (self-esteem), the more self-confidence you will have. Self-esteem is perhaps the biggest factor in determining our happiness. If we aren't happy with who we are, this unhappiness manifests in every area of our lives. Although certainly not the only determinant of happiness, self-esteem is considered among the most important. If you are a Goddess who has some work to do in this area, there is good news. Self-esteem can be cultivated by acknowledging what is good and right about you, and by focusing your attention on those strengths and positive attributes.

Self-esteem relates to the extent to which you see yourself as valuable and worthy. When you have healthy self-esteem, you feel good about yourself and believe you deserve the respect of others. When you have low self-esteem, you put little value on your opinions and ideas. You might constantly worry you aren't good enough. Stated another way, self-esteem is the extent to which you appreciate yourself through an honest and accurate assessment.[26] Self-esteem fluctuates – it is rare for an individual to float consistently through life with high self-esteem – but overall, it should be relatively stable. We are amazing Goddess beings with an endless ability to learn, create, and love, and we have the right to feel good about ourselves. It is my hope that in this chapter you will gain insight into the powerful role self-esteem plays in our lives and that you will use the techniques, information and tools to feel better about yourself in those "down times" that periodically affect us all.

Imagine a linear scale divided into four sections. On the far right, we see high self-esteem; then, to the left, moderate self-esteem; then low self-esteem; and at the far left side, self-dislike:

Self-Esteem			
Self-Dislike	**Low**	**Moderate**	**High**

The negative health manifestations that can accompany self-dislike and low self-esteem are many and can be severe. Low self-esteem leads to chronic depression, anxiety, alcohol and drug abuse, promiscuity, eating disorders, dependency, and social difficulties. Based on this list, I am sure you agree that moving closer to the high end of the self-esteem spectrum as quickly as possible is critical in order to circumvent the potential for these catastrophic symptoms and the feelings they inflict upon us.

---

[26] Schiraldi, G. (2001). *The Self-Esteem Workbook*

Building Self-Esteem

We learn self-esteem in our family of origin; we do not inherit it. It is an inside-out job that answers the question, "How do I feel about who I am?" Self-esteem begins to form in early childhood, when we define ourselves by how other people react to us. It grows or shrinks with experiences at home, in school and, in later years, at work. Sometimes it is affected by our role and status in society, or by messages from the media.

Relationships with those close to us – siblings, peers, teachers and, of course, parents – are important to self-esteem. The beliefs we hold today are the accumulation of messages received over time. If relationships have been strong and we have received generally positive feedback, we're more likely to see ourselves as worthwhile and have healthier self-esteem. If we received mostly negative feedback and were often criticized, teased, or devalued by others, we're more likely to struggle with poor self-esteem.

Brené Brown, a research professor and expert on vulnerability, shame, and authenticity, teaches how to deconstruct why we attach our self-worth to outside forces.[27] One of the books I purchased during my own transformational work was Brown's *The Gifts of Imperfection*.[28] The ten "guideposts" she offers to support transforming our self-image mirror the Goddess Essence Code nicely, as well as the teachings throughout this book. I appreciate the way Brown has tied the attribute we need to bring more of into our life with what we need to let go of to support its cultivation.

- Authenticity by letting go of what others think
- Self-compassion by letting go of perfectionism
- A resilient spirit by letting go of numbness and powerlessness
- Gratitude and joy by letting go of scarcity and fear of the dark

---

[27] http://brenebrown.com/
[28] Book can be ordered from my website: http://transformingvenus.com/product-category/books/

- Intuition and faith by letting go of the need for certainty
- Creativity by letting go of comparison
- Play and rest by letting go of exhaustion as a status symbol and productivity as self-worth
- Calm and stillness by letting go of anxiety as a lifestyle
- Meaningful work by letting go of self-doubt
- Laughter and fun by letting go of the need to be cool and always in control

How do we do all this? If you are working through the chapters of this book and completing the exercises, you are already on track in cultivating these attributes.

You will also notice this chapter has a few more exercises than other chapters, as it is the area many stuck Goddesses find most challenging. Completing these exercises honestly will go a long way toward improving self-esteem, but you will need to practice the new behaviors each and every day. NOW is the time to put more emphasis and attention on our own needs and wants. I'm not talking about being selfish, but consciously considering our own needs first. Why do you think they tell you to put your own oxygen mask on first while flying? We can't help others in need if we ourselves are in a weakened state. Listening carefully to what our heart, mind, and body are telling us is a good first step.

It is important to remember we have innate Divine Feminine Wisdom within us. If our thoughts tell us that new person we just met is going to drain our energy reserves, we need to listen and act accordingly – basically, ditch them! If our body, through neck or back discomfort, tells us we have been sitting too long, we need to get up off of our butt and spend a few moments bending and stretching! If our heart tells us we have been neglecting good friends, we need to get a plan together to connect with them as soon as possible! Ignoring these messages does not a happy and healthy Goddess make! Acting on these messages helps us realize we do have the confidence to know what is best for us, and we have accomplished things of which we can be proud.

I invite you to reward yourself for all the positive steps you have taken so far to boost your self-esteem. Why not indulge in a luxurious bubble bath or take some extra time out for a positive affirmations meditation? The reward is your choice: a fun romantic comedy movie, or something else you would enjoy and feel even better because of it – another win-win experience!

 ## Exercise: Goddess Greatness

In this exercise, I invite you to reflect back on some of your accomplishments, ones you are particularly proud of and admire yourself for. Then complete the following statements, or modify them to create five new statements with the same goal in mind: celebrating your Goddess Greatness.

1. I admire myself for

   _____

2. I am proud of myself for

   _____

3. Yay me! I did it!

   _____

4. It was a challenge, but I managed to

   _____

5. WOW! I am so happy I accomplished

   _____

I'm sure you could come up with even more things you are proud of, accomplishments you have achieved, and things you admire yourself for doing. Do you feel your self-esteem rising? What is holding you back from doing something else that will make you feel good about yourself? Oh yes – only yourself! Past behavior is indicative of future behavior. You have done it before, and you can do it again! You may have heard the saying "Man Up," meaning to be tough enough to deal with the situation.

 I am going to modify that slightly and say, "Goddess Up," similarly meaning to step up and *get 'er done!* Like the Shania Twain song lyrics say – *let's go, girls!*

 ## Exercise: Goddess Goodies

List some examples of goodies (rewards or treats) you deserve (yes, you do deserve them) for the work you have done to date. Consider rewards that don't cost any money. Consider marrying the results of your passions, dreams, and goals with this exercise once you have completed Chapters 15, 16 and 17 related to this content.

_____   _____   _____

_____   _____   _____

_____   _____   _____

_____   _____   _____

_____   _____   _____

Exercise: Goddess Giggle

They say laughter is the best medicine. With that in mind, make a list of ten things you can do to support bringing forth your Goddess giggle!

_____   _____

_____   _____

_____   _____

_____   _____

_____   _____

Journaling Exercise: Goddess Self-Esteem

Create a dedicated space in your journal for this exercise and continue to document on a daily basis for at least one full week. Keep your journal nearby and, in this dedicated area, write down every negative thought you have about yourself as it arises. Next to the negative thought, indicate what triggered it. For instance, if the thought related to your weight, what made you think of it? Did you pass a mirror and notice your figure? Did you eat a second helping and then think of your weight? Did someone close to you say something related to your weight? Did you hang your sweatshirt over the handles on the side of your treadmill and notice it was dusty?

After one week of documenting all negative thoughts, review your journal for patterns. This critical review will provide you with the details you need to create a plan for overcoming these negative thoughts and thereby overcoming low self-esteem.

 # Exercise: Three Adjectives

For some positive reinforcement (which we all need from time to time), you may want to ask some of your Goddess girlfriends and family members to answer a simple question for you. Using email, private messaging, or good old-fashioned person-to-person communication, ask them to complete the following exercise:

1. Ask 20 people to respond to you with the first three adjectives that come to their mind to describe you. Do not give them examples, as this causes bias.
2. Create a numbered list, 1-20, either in a typed file or in your journal. As you receive the responses from each person, document them on the next line available (e.g. Creative, Loving, Fun). Do not change the words in any way.

3. When all responses are back, use the highlighting option in your software (or different colored highlighters, if you used your journal) to group similar words together. Yellow could be kind or kind-hearted or kindness – whatever people have said. Green could be used to highlight another category of descriptors.

4. Now take a look at your fully color-coded list and see what words come to mind most often.

You should get a pretty good picture of how positively people see you. Don't dwell on any words you don't understand or disagree with, and **do not** go back and ask people for clarification. These are simply the three words that came to their mind when thinking of you; questioning them further is not part of the exercise. **Do** go back one more time to reflect on the positive responses, and then reflect on any results that offer potential opportunities for improvement. This exercise usually provides a real boost of self-esteem as you see yourself in a new light – through the eyes of others.

As you use this new knowledge and the tools offered to support you in boosting your self-esteem, you will start to feel better about yourself. You will notice you are enjoying yourself more often than when you first set out on this journey. You will also find you are challenging yourself more often with new and different things, and accomplishing more of the goals you had for your life with those dreams and passions embedded into them.

With self-esteem being a key indicator to health and happiness, I say *yes* to making a concerted effort to put more energy and effort into overcoming potentially low self-esteem. What say you, Goddess?

Positive Affirmations Related to Self-Esteem:

- I am congruent in all I say and do.
- I see the best in myself and my efforts.
- I recognize the many good qualities I possess.
- I focus on positive thoughts and feelings about myself.
- I believe in me.

Chapter 11

Cultivating Mindful Self-Compassion

"If your compassion does not include yourself, it is incomplete." *Jack Kornfield*

Goddess Tenet #8: A Goddess has a responsibility to respect herself as a sacred being, and to take care of her needs in the physical, sexual, mental, and spiritual sense.

Goddess Jaqueline, age 47, from Nice, France tells her story:
Self-compassion means being kind to yourself. It means accepting yourself just the way you are and not judging yourself for your imperfections. Practicing self-compassion involves resolving not to suffer silently, but to care for yourself with the same love and understanding you would offer to a friend, family member, or animal during challenging times.

Throughout my life as an actress and writer, I have always found it so easy to be compassionate toward others, but so very difficult to be compassionate with myself. I am a giver. Receiving compassion was a very foreign concept. That all changed when Valentine, a thousand-pound rescue horse, galloped into my life.

It was a crisp fall day in southern Nice as I drove up the long driveway leading to my friend's horse ranch. Understanding that it was important for me to "unplug" now and again, I was looking forward to spending some quiet time feeding apples and carrots to a few of my friend's horses. My inner critic had been very loud, as of late, constantly reminding me of what I needed to do and especially what I had not yet accomplished in my career and personal life. The dark circles under my eyes were a clue that I was not sleeping well, lying awake in the middle of night, fretting over finances and next steps. Other dialogue included asking myself, "Where is my life going? How could I have made such stupid choices that clearly caused me to go backwards instead of forward?"

After making the rounds, a herd of rescue horses in the upper pasture caught my eye and I was drawn to visit them, too. As I walked up to the pasture, some of the horses came up to the fence to say hello, but I noticed one particular horse, a timid, long-legged mare, who stayed back, wary of my presence. I said hello to her in a soft voice. She looked at me for a moment, and then put her head down.

The next time I visited the ranch, I brought extra apples and carrots for the rescue horses. They were so excited about their treats and all of them hugged the fence, save the long-legged mare. She hung back. Again, I spoke to her in a soft voice, and slowly and gently extended my hand toward her. When she didn't come up to the fence, I didn't push. I just sat on the fence and talked to her softly. I repeated this pattern during the next four or five visits until, one sunny day, she got just close enough to the fence that I could reach out and touch her sweet face. At first, she drew back, but then she dropped her head forward so I could give her a scratch under her chin. I was elated with this victory!

As I scratched Valentine's chin, I realized I was very much like her – wary, hanging back, not allowing myself to feel the love and kindness I so desperately needed.

The following week, I went into the pasture with a soft brush and comb. I approached the mare slowly, showing her the brush and comb, and asked her if I could brush her coat and mane. Ever so gently and slowly I brushed her, getting rid of all the old, matted hair on her back, and combed through the tangles in her mane. As the sun beamed down on her, she closed her eyes and relaxed. I remember that moment of pure tranquility. My heart felt full. I had eased the suffering of this gentle giant, by offering her love and kindness.

I decided to apply the same compassion I had offered Valentine to myself. I always spoke softly to her, so I started to speak softly to myself. I never pushed Valentine to do anything she didn't want to do, so I stopped pushing myself to do things that caused me grief. I surrounded myself with a herd of friends who treated me with kindness and listened to me without judgment. I scheduled time for self-care and made a point of basking in the sunshine. I recognized my accomplishments, understanding that like Valentine, who was once a racehorse, sometimes bad things happen that are not in your control and starting over is the only option. And starting over can be very good, once you move out of the fear of the unknown.

Valentine taught me that I was expecting myself to win the "race" every time as an actress, writer, daughter, partner, and friend. I had abandoned my SELF and my self-compassion. Once I started to practice self-compassion, things in my life started to shift. I no longer "yell" at myself or question my choices. Rather, I allow myself to take each day as it comes, knowing that the more I practice self-compassion, the more I will have to give.

Valentine now shares a beautiful pasture with another horse and is peaceful and content. She is a testament of what compassion can do and a reminder of what self-compassion can do for you and me.

* * *

We can boost our self-confidence and build our self-esteem, but they will not stay fortified if we do not add one more ingredient: self-compassion. In order to stay on the path of personal development, and to reap the benefits of high self-confidence and self-esteem, we must learn to love ourselves. Don't worry about what comes first out of this essential triad; they all work in harmony, and all must be cultivated.

Whilst loving ourselves is one of the most often repeated pieces of advice, it is also one of the most obscure. After all, what does it really mean to be self-compassionate? Is it as simple as redirecting negative thoughts in a gentle way? To me, self-compassion is one of the most difficult qualities to integrate, yet the most worthwhile on this journey of personal growth.

Let's start exploring where we can have more compassion for ourselves by looking at something we are all very familiar with: the inner critic.

The Inner Critic

> "Pay no attention to what the critics say. A statue has never been erected in honor of a critic." *Jean Sibelius*

Our inner critic is that pesky part of our ego that supposedly protects us from ourselves; yet sometimes it can pummel us with negativity. It is time to give that occupant its eviction notice! I'm not suggesting we shouldn't reflect on our behavior, but we need to do so with loving kindness. Keep any encountered setbacks in perspective. Recognize that mistakes represent problem-solving opportunities, providing important moments of positive self-growth and the inherent happiness that goes along with them.

 Our ultimate goal is to let our inner wisdom guide us, not the inner critic.

In your transformational journey you will need to bust through some disempowering beliefs, fears, doubts, and self-imposed limitations. Similarly, if self-sabotage is a negative pattern you struggle with, now is a good time to put your female wisdom to use. Make a concerted effort to stop doubt-filled and other negative thoughts and feelings in their tracks!

How does one do this? It's simple in theory, but takes some practice to master. As a negative or self-deflating thought percolates and enters our thought field, we need to consciously state a one-syllable word such as "stop" or "cease" or some other word signaling the need to redirect the thought. Then, immediately replace the thought with a positive and affirming thought. The goal is to refuse these lower living, ego-driven put-downs to enter our Goddess mind space. We need to treat ourselves well – every day! We need to infuse our daily existence with Goddess self-appreciation, self-acceptance, and inner pride. Those with self-esteem know how to love from a secure home base – from within.

Self-Compassion

It is a well-known fact that there is a positive correlation between the positive quality of our thoughts and the increased level of happiness we feel; yet many women habitually criticize and judge themselves in the harshest of ways. I call this judgment crew "the itty bitty shitty committee" (or IBSC). This is the negative forum inside our heads that loves and feeds on the drama, the pain, and the crap we pile on ourselves. The IBSC holds us back by filling our heads with lies, causing us to beat ourselves up over our inadequacies and ineptness at dealing with the challenges we face in life. Rather than berating ourselves for our parenting style or relationships and various life choices, we need to create a caring, judgment-free space.

There is no arguing that life can be tough at times. Sickness, death, financial stress, relationship struggles and breakups, work stressors, children challenges (even into their adulthood), parent challenges, you name it – they can all affect our lives at any time, sometimes many of them at once. Compounding the everyday stressors, there are mentalities such as "keeping up with the Jones" where we want what others have (material possessions, power, wealth, a perfect figure, etc.).

We have created a competitive society where the norm is to judge, evaluate, and compare ourselves on a constant basis. We are bombarded with messages (some more subtle than others) through TV, magazines, and other media, telling us what we should and shouldn't have, what we ought to do and not do, what we need and don't need, often leaving us confused and wanting. Add to this our nurturing-to-a-fault natures, supporting others to the point where we have left little or nothing for ourselves.

 As we learned in chapter 7, we need to stop "should-ing" on ourselves.

We Goddesses fear, judge, criticize, dislike, and avoid more than any other species. These inherently negative emotions and behaviors are regularly directed at – you guessed it – ourselves! How is it that we can value being kind, considerate, and nurturing to others, but be so hard and uncaring toward ourselves? Often, there is no other person we are more unkind to than ourselves.

We can learn to deal with the barrage of challenges without beating ourselves up with the mental banter that regularly marches through our minds. Making an effort to get a handle on our self-talk and greeting this emotional suffering with acceptance, kindness, and caring will go a long way to help us bounce back from life's challenges. Self-compassion can shorten the recovery time when dealing with relationship and marriage breakups, poor body image, work-related challenges, and dependency issues (food, sex, alcohol, drugs).

Professional help may be needed to support us with these challenges, but ultimately … you guessed it!

 Cultivating self-compassion is another inside job!

Self-compassion is all about giving ourselves the same loving kindness we would give a friend in need – being kind and understanding with ourselves when we make mistakes or something happens that we may not be ready for or want. It includes being open to our own suffering and not trying to avoid or disconnect from it – lovingly embracing it, so that moving forward is possible.

Life will continue to throw us curveballs, frustrations will occur, and we will make mistakes; but we were not meant to be perfect. We are here to learn and grow, and to experience life as an adventure. The more we accept our shortcomings and all the inevitable bumps in life, the easier it will be for us to practice self-compassion.

Being kind, considerate, and caring to others while judging and criticizing ourselves at every turn does not a happy Goddess make. We deserve kindness, too. A lot of us have never given any thought to the fact that we are actually allowed to be nice to ourselves. In fact, it's highly encouraged and necessary, making us a lot more fun to be around. It also brings us closer to a life with more bliss – something we all desire!

Moreover, a growing body of research links self-compassion with psychological health.[29] Those with higher levels of self-compassion have much sought-after traits that the rest of us want more of, such as happiness, curiosity, the desire to explore, initiative, optimism, social connectedness, and emotional intelligence. Improvements across other issues, including anger, depression, stress, anxiety, self-criticism, and eating disorders, have been observed in those with self-compassion. It has also been proven that self-compassion plays a major role in how people face life's problems. People who are self-compassionate suffer less and have greater life satisfaction than those who lack in it.[30] Individuals with high levels of self-compassion are also more likely to experience positive feelings because they accept themselves the way they are, resulting in less friction and stress when facing life's inevitable challenges.

---

[29] http://self-compassion.org/wp-content/uploads/2015/08/Finlay_Jones.pdf
[30] http://self-compassion.org/wp-content/uploads/publications/SC_SE_Well_being.pdf

I believe most women our age were taught to put the needs of others before our own. I repeatedly heard various chants when I was growing up like, "It's not all about me," and, "Don't be so selfish," and these thoughts were ingrained in my brain. I think many of us might have picked up a common disempowering belief that self-compassion is a weakness akin to being soft or letting ourselves off the hook. The reality is that the opposite is true – self-compassion is not a weakness; it is an act of courage. Courage to face up to the challenges we face, including our failures and screw-ups – courage to dissect the emotions and feelings caused by these situations. This creates awareness and kindness, whereby we accept the fact that we are human.

Self-compassion is not about making suffering disappear; it is about being with our thoughts and feelings in a non-judgmental, kind, and loving way. Kristin Neff, PhD and pioneering researcher on self-compassion, has developed a three-prong approach that includes self-kindness, a sense of common humanity, and mindfulness to help us process the elements of self-compassion.[31]

Self-Kindness

Self-kindness includes caring for our own wellbeing. This may require us to deal with a situation (addiction or behavior) that we know is not good for us and needs attention. It bids us to show concern and be nice to ourselves, to show the same sympathy (being moved by a person's plight), empathy (identifying mentally with and thereby comprehending a person's situation), and appreciation (understanding of their dilemma) toward our self that we regularly show to others.

---

[31] http://self-compassion.org/the-three-elements-of-self-compassion-2/#3elements

Common Humanity

More often than not, when we're in the thick of uncomfortable situations and emotional distress, we feel isolated and alone. Recognizing our common humanity helps us realize that all of us suffer from time to time and we are not alone. We need to begin to see our challenges as part of the universal life experience of being human.

Mindfulness

This element of self-compassion involves making sure we hold our painful thoughts, negative feelings, and emotions in balance. We need to be mindful that we are not over-identifying and exaggerating them, or blowing them out of proportion. Conversely, we also do not want to under-identify or suppress them, thereby not giving them the attention they deserve. Taking a good look at others who are also suffering is a realistic way to find balance by putting our own situation into perspective.

Using Mindfulness to Cultivate Compassion

For years, mindfulness was commonly associated with the Buddhist tradition and practice. It has evolved to become a commonly used foundational tool to support emotional healing.

As discussed in chapter four, mindful self-compassion involves being aware in the present moment. It includes giving non-judgmental attention to our thoughts when we are struggling with difficult emotions, and responding to ourselves with loving awareness and kindness. This practice leads to better coping skills and improved wellbeing. Mindfulness is a key component of meditation as well, although you don't have to meditate to practice mindfulness.

Benefits of mindfulness include improved concentration and mental clarity, calmness, enhanced self-control, emotional intelligence, and the ability to relate to others and one's self with caring, kindness, honesty, acceptance, and non-judgment. Sounds like the components of compassion to me!

 ## Exercise: Love and Compassion Meditation

Close your eyes and picture yourself relaxing in a magnificently comfy chair in a peaceful, blissful environment. You may see yourself sitting in your elegantly furnished oceanfront condo in Panama with the waves gently rolling onto the shore, or you may see yourself sitting in your comfortable rocking chair that you rocked your children and perhaps grandchildren in, strategically placed in front of a large bay window to overlook the wildlife that regularly visits your cottage in the woods. Find your own visual "happy place."

Breathe in and out, with your eyes closed. As thoughts come to mind, regardless of what they are, do not judge them. Simply let them enter, and then pass through. Don't stick with any one thought. Remain fully aware of the thoughts, emotions, and sensations that arise, but make a practice of not reacting to them. Simply observe those thoughts and feelings as they are in the present moment. No drama, no criticism. This pleasant mindful state is a good place to start to support you in building more self-compassion. As you breathe in, say to yourself, "Love and compassion for me," and as you exhale say to yourself, "Love and compassion for others." Sit quietly for a minimum of 15 minutes completing this exercise.

 ## Exercise: Guided Self-Compassion Meditation

Here is a link to seven guided medications on self-compassion, compliments of Kristin Neff. They range in length from 7-24 minutes. http://self-compassion.org/category/exercises/#guided-meditations

Download them to your phone or computer and listen to them during times of need, or at any time to cultivate a more self-compassionate resonance.

 ## Exercise: Self-Compassion

The next time you find yourself doubting, questioning, criticizing or beating yourself up about a situation (and that time may be now), ask yourself these four **yes** or **no** response questions:

1. Is this a kind and loving way to portray myself?   Y N
2. Would I be dishing out this same message to a good friend?   Y N
3. Is what I am telling myself really true?   Y N
4. Is this self-talk positive and helpful to my situation?   Y N

If you answered the majority of these questions with a *no*, it is time to find a new way to approach your situation(s).

 ## Journaling Exercise: Cultivating Self-Compassion

This exercise contains three components. Please complete all three in your journal.

1. Write about an issue you are facing that makes you feel bad about yourself. It is important to consider this matter deeply. Bringing it out into the open will ensure you are not simply repressing and therefore not dealing with the matter.

   First, write about the crux of the issue (what happened, who was involved). Then write about how this makes you feel. What emotions come to the surface? Write about these emotions and why you believe you feel the way you do. Be honest and forthright in documenting your issues and feelings.

2. Once your writing is done, think about your new best friend – your journal – as a person. She is kind, unconditionally loving, accepting, and full of compassion. Let's call her Journella. She knows your SHIT because you have been honest and forthright with her, and you have told her all your secrets and deepest thoughts. Sit back and think about her loving feelings for you, and how she is non-judgmental and only wants to help you grow as a person. She knows the good, the bad, and the ugly. She knows your strengths, your weaknesses, and the skeletons in your closet.

    But she loves you because, despite all you beat yourself up about, she knows everyone has a host of human imperfections and everyone makes mistakes. She knows life is a journey and we all get a little off track at times. She knows we have all done stuff we aren't proud of. We are human beings and we are on a journey of learning – failure, screw-ups, and imperfection are all part of the ride. Journella recognizes the limits of human nature and knows what you have been through in this life (and perhaps previous ones) to bring you to this current moment. She is kind and forgiving toward you; and more than anything, she wants you to be kind and forgiving toward yourself.

3. Now, acting as Journella, write a letter to yourself in your journal, focusing on what she wants to convey about the pain she feels when you judge yourself so harshly and how you need to work at feeding yourself heaping doses, not just baby spoonfuls, of this compassion medicine. As you write to yourself from Journella's perspective, infuse your letter with a strong sense of her love, acceptance, kindness, and caring,

and her very real desire for your health and bliss. She wants this for you.

4. When this writing exercise is complete, turn the page and leave this exercise alone. In a few days, return and read over the letter that you, as Journella, wrote to yourself – perhaps even a few times, so you really get the feel for the compassion directed toward yourself. From this moment forward, every time your mind starts with negative self-talk or unkind thoughts, think about the positive, kind, and gentle messages Journella shared with you and what she wants for you. Start acting like your own best friend!

 ## Exercise: Self-Compassion Reflection

Answer the following questions in the space provided, or in your journal.

1. Think about a recent situation when you felt bad about yourself or struggled with a situation you were dealing with. How did you respond to yourself?

   _____

   _____

   _____

   _____

   What was the advice you gave to yourself?

   _____

   _____

   _____

   _____

Describe your tone and communication style.

_____

_____

_____

_____

2. Now, think about a recent situation when a good friend felt bad about her/himself or struggled with a situation. How did you respond to your friend?

_____

_____

_____

_____

What advice did you give them?

_____

_____

_____

_____

Describe your tone and communication style.

_____

_____

_____

_____

3. What, if any, difference did you notice in the approach, advice, tone, and communication style in the two different instances? If you did notice any differences, consider the contributing factors that might have precipitated treating yourself differently from others.

_____

_____

_____

_____

4. Document the changes you could expect if you responded to yourself in the same manner you typically adopt when responding to a close friend, when you yourself are suffering.

_____

_____

_____

_____

 Begin to treat yourself like a close friend, and see what it feels like to receive empathy and kindness when you need it most.

Positive Affirmations Related to Self-Compassion:

- My life is getting easier as I practice cultivating moments of self-compassion.
- I am a loving human being. I am not perfect, nor do I need to be.
- I am on a learning journey. I am exactly where I need to be today.
- I am gentle with myself, feeling what I need to feel and then letting it go without judgment.

Chapter 12

Practicing a Caring Approach to Health and Wellness

"To keep the body in good health is a duty ... otherwise, we shall not be able to keep our mind strong and clear." *The Buddha*

Goddess Tenet #8: A Goddess has a responsibility to respect herself as a sacred being, and to take care of her needs in the physical, sexual, mental, and spiritual sense.

Goddess Jessica, age 62, from Barcelona, Spain shares her story:

If you are anything like me, you are a woman who cares deeply about being and expressing your best self. And yet life seems to play a cruel trick on us as we age. Just as we are in the prime of our lives, we notice our bodies begin to change and symptoms appear. This has certainly been true for me. I believe we all have had lessons to learn through the fire of bodily challenges. For me, I have had to learn how to be healthy and feel balanced in my body. My health journey and struggle through the years has given me a burning passion to inspire others to achieve and experience a healthy, balanced, and vibrant body at any age.

It all started in my 20s. While attending grad school, I recognized I was addicted to sugar. I had to develop tremendous fortitude to overcome this. Sugar cravings have every bit as much power, control, and hold over the human body as alcohol or drugs. It wasn't easy, but I was determined to kick the sugar habit and never again be controlled by an outside substance.

In my early 30s, while traveling on business one night, someone broke into my hotel room and assaulted me badly. I sold my business to focus on healing my body just to be able to function normally. I learned how painful the journey to restored health and wellness can be, and what it takes to commit to this goal.

Through this healing process I was blessed with meeting a wonderful man. We eventually married and had a daughter. But life tossed me a curve ball and I ended up having three miscarriages, all taking a tremendous toll on my body. Again, my body needed to heal.

In my despair, I never gave up hope. I kept seeing what I wanted – a vibrant, healthy body and the ability to have another child. I was determined and held onto the mental attitude that it was possible. I pictured it, felt it, and visualized that I already had what I wanted. I believed it in my soul. Just as I had imagined, I had another healthy baby girl at the age of 42.

I hummed along in my 40s and then I hit a wall again. There I was, entering my 50s, when my body began to go through unpleasant changes and shifts I could no longer control. It was a bleak time. My body had already endured so much, overcoming difficult challenges and painful lessons. And yet there I was again being tested on the physical level, losing that precious feeling of a healthy, balanced body. No matter how well I ate, how much I exercised, meditated, and supplemented with nutritional products, I could not improve my health. I was frustrated, discouraged, and suffering.

The joy and zest I used to feel about life began to wane, and misery clouded over my normally sunny disposition. I had terrible inflammation in my hands and feet, was sleeping terribly, my digestive system felt like it was shutting down, and I lacked the energy and mental clarity to get through my busy days. My skin began to age and I was looking old and tired, like a dry, wrinkled prune. I felt like a prisoner in my own body. I was desperate and miserable.

My husband would say to me, "This is just normal aging. You had better get used to it, as this is going to be your new normal." "No," I replied emphatically. I fought his suggestion with every nerve and bone in my body. I felt there had to be an answer. We are not meant to feel like that as we age.

I asked myself many times, "Why I am I having so many traumatic life lessons come through my body? What do I need to learn?" With deep reflection, I have come to this profound realization: my soul (spirit) loves me so much that it has used my body to get my attention. Yes, that's right. I needed something dramatic and intense in order for me to stop, reflect, and change direction when I was off track in my soul's journey. When I needed to correct how I was living or be better aligned with my life purpose, my soul used my body to get my attention. So often I wasn't listening to the signals or heeding the warning signs that I was off-balance or not taking care of myself properly. Most of all, I was holding onto unexpressed, repressed emotions that would then manifest in bodily challenges.

Once I realized this, I began to listen more carefully – more attentively – to the subtle signs of my body. I no longer have to be "hit over the head" to self-correct when I need to make soul adjustments in my life. I now have daily self-care routines in place and I can live in my body more effortlessly. I have more flow, and see my body as the true temple that it is.

I also wondered, "Is it really possible to have a younger feeling body as I age? Can I feel a vital, healthy sense of wellbeing into my later years? Do I have to accept disease as the only option for my journey into the golden years?"

Science is beginning to understand that the aging process begins inside our 50 trillion cells. And if we can give our body what it needs to stop aging, both mentally and physically, we can become healthier in every cell – period.

It all starts with how we think. We can change how we think about our bodies as we age, to shift our expectations. I am now more mindful of what I think, the words that I say, and how I treat my body. I also give my body the proper nutrients and food to help it thrive. I have never felt healthier. I walk, hike, do yoga, take spin classes, do weight-bearing exercises, dance, and do it all with gratitude for being able to enjoy moving my body, for the pleasure it brings me.

I am living proof that it is possible to look and feel fabulous at any age.

* * *

Until this chapter, we have focused on the inner work it takes to transform our Goddess selves. While I believe it is more effective to "work our way out," transforming from inside to outside, this does not mean we should neglect our physical selves. Our minds and bodies are connected, and if we want to feel our best mentally and be balanced emotionally, we must take good care of our physical bodies. Fatigue and stress easily lead back to the feelings associated with being restless and stuck. While all the inner work we have been talking about will alleviate these feelings, if you really want to kick-start your transformation, and allow all the personal development work you are doing to have maximum effect, balance it with a healthy physical wellness practice. Those instances when I have felt amazing in my physical body, either after a great day of eating right or a good workout, I have felt infinitely calmer, balanced, and resilient.

The content in this chapter is based on my own physical practice, as well as research into what women approaching (or already in the throes of) menopause need to pay attention to. The goal of this chapter is to provide you with information that will help guide you in taking a caring approach to your health and wellness. A variety of techniques for you to add to your Goddess health and wellness toolkit are included. This will equip you to begin incorporating some of these choices into your life.

I have focused on a holistic approach to health and wellness through a combination of nutritional tips, ideas for getting more active, nutrient supplements, and an energy technique that will support your health and wellness goals. Good nutrition and small lifestyle changes will go a long way in supporting you in good health, into, through and beyond menopause.

A Nutritional Balancing Act

Gone are the days when we grew our own vegetables and raised our own livestock. Over the last 50 years, the rise in fast food restaurants and production of processed foods has reached epic proportions. Our food chain has been negatively modified with the addition of herbicides, pesticides, antibiotics (used to prevent the spread of disease due to more animals produced in less space), preservatives, and growth hormones. It's hard to know what is safe to eat and what foods are affected by these components – and who has time to figure it all out? As a result, most of us now have genetically modified foods in our kitchens.

We live in a fast-paced world today, and it is increasingly commonly for women to manage both a job and the household. This puts a heavy burden on the modern woman. It's no wonder healthy eating is taking the hit. We're always in a hurry, and there is such a wide variety of processed and fast foods available – even "organic" and "natural" versions – that it's easier to buy these than to prepare a full meal from scratch. After all, we "deserve a break today," as a previous *McDonald's* restaurant slogan boasted for 43 years.

 We *do* need a break – but fast food is not the solution!

Marketing companies have done an admirable job of selling us on the need for all those helpful pre-packaged, ready-to-eat meals as our lives have become complicated with jobs, kids, and other commitments – but at what cost? We bought these products because we were so busy. We didn't have the time or the wherewithal to investigate the nutritional value (or lack thereof) and production intricacies of each and every item. We were busy – hence the need for these solutions in the first place!

 To coin a phrase (and the pun is intended) – we ate it all up!

The Internet has certainly provided an easier way to learn more about nutrition and health, but it takes time to find the most trusted resources and sort through the information.

 Yes, there are many .con sites to sift through to get to valid .com ones.

In short, proper nutrition has become a balancing act of sorts, requiring us to put some time and effort into determining the best choices to maintain our best health. But it's worth it, because good nutrition can assist us in feeling better. Let's take a look at how good food choices can help boost our bliss.

Boost Your Bliss by Eating for Your Health

Although I am not a physician, I have spent 23 years working in the information management side of health care, including training in biomedical science and research, so I am well aware of the choices we need to make to maintain good health. You too may already know some of this, but sometimes we need a reminder to get us back on track with full participation. After all, as our bodies change, so do our nutritional needs.

It's easy to feel overwhelmed by all the information available about eating a "healthy and "well-balanced" diet, and some of it is contradictory. At the end of the day, keep it simple. All we really need to do is eat food; and the simpler, more natural your food is, the better.

Strike List

Here is a list of items you should make an attempt to reduce, or strike altogether from your food regime:

- caffeine
- white sugar
- salt
- alcohol
- deli meats
- margarine
- fried foods

Although caffeine is on the strike list, you can add green tea to your regime. Green tea is highly renowned as being beneficial to our health in lots of ways. For example, it is packed with anti-oxidants and is even believed to be a weight-loss aid.

It's helpful to get into the habit of drinking more water daily. You may know the average human body is between 50-75% water,[32] and we have all heard we should drink up to eight 8-ounce glasses a day. If you drink this much already, you might be thinking you should cut back on your water consumption, especially if you would like to lose 10-20 pounds.

 This is not a good idea. Why? Because the water you drink literally becomes you!

Water is critical for muscle and skin tone, lubrication of joints, eliminating toxins and wastes from our bodies, transporting nutrients and oxygen to our cells, healthy cell reproduction, and the regulation of body temperature.[33]

---

[32] Chemistry.about.com/od/waterchemistry/f/How-Much-Of-Your-Body-Is-Water.htm

[33] Chemistry.about.com/od/waterchemistry/f/How-Much-Of-Your-Body-Is-Water.htm

If you are menopausal, regulating your body temperature in the face of those hot flashes probably sounds pretty good, right about now.

These are just some of the most basic changes you can make to start a new regime of healthy eating. You might also want to experiment with the Mediterranean diet, touted for its simplicity, the use of fresh ingredients, and a lack of deep-frying or over-cooking methods.

Simple, fresh, whole – keeping an eye out for real food, nothing packaged and processed – is really all it takes to start eating well. The bigger challenge lies in shifting your mindset to one where you acknowledge it takes exactly the same amount of time to prepare a healthy, hearty salad as it does to heat up that packaged entrée you brought home. It will always be worth the commitment.

Necessary Nutrients to Support Bone Health through Midlife

Most of us are aware that the estrogen hormone is important in our sexual development as budding Goddesses, including supporting pregnancy and childbirth as we became mothering Goddesses. Many of us may not be aware how extensive the role of estrogen is within our bodies. Around the age of 30, our bone replacement and new bone growth capabilities begin to slow, and our bodies no longer make more bone than they rebuild.[34] This is directly related to a decline in estrogen production, which is inevitable in perimenopause and menopausal years.

Our bones are filled with collagen and calcium, among other minerals. Calcium is responsible for making our bones strong and rigid. As we age, the decline in estrogen accelerates the loss of calcium from our bones, which increases our risk of developing osteoarthritis,

---

[34] http://www.healthywomen.org/condition/estrogen

a progressive deterioration of bone density and mass.[35] Estrogen plays a role in the absorption of calcium from food; so when estrogen levels fall, the body absorbs calcium less efficiently. Calcium is therefore particularly important around menopause. If you are not getting the recommended calcium you need from your diet, ask your physician about adding calcium supplements to assist in slowing the rate of bone loss and the risk of fractures. According to the National Osteoporosis Foundation, women under 50 should take 1,000 milligrams per day, and women over 50 should take 1,200 milligrams per day,[36] further stating "too many Americans fall short of getting the amount of calcium they need every day, and that can lead to bone loss, low bone density, and even broken bones."

Vitamin D is essential for the absorption of calcium, so it is also an important vitamin in bone strength and health. Sunshine is our greatest friend when it comes to this vitamin. All we need is about 15 minutes per day, several times per week, on our hands, arms, and face. With this, the body can make enough vitamin D to get us through the winter months. However, with increased concerns about skin cancer, most of us use sun protection. National Osteoporosis Foundation research shows that even a low SPF, such as SPF 8, reduces our production of vitamin D by as much as 95%.[37] Although vitamin D is found in some foods, like egg yolks, fortified milk products, salmon, beef liver, and sardines canned in oil, the reality is many of us need a supplement of this necessary vitamin. Women under 50 need 400-800 international units (IU) per day and those over 50 need 800-1,000 IU.[38]

Before adding this or any other supplement to your diet, please check with your physician or healthcare practitioner as part of a medically supervised healthcare plan. Check your other vitamin

---

[35] http://orthoinfo.aaos.org/topic.cfm?topic=a00127

[36] http://nof.org/calcium

[37] http://nof.org/calcium#howmuchvitamind

[38] http://nof.org/calcium#howmuchvitamind

supplements to see if they too have a Vitamin D component, as often calcium supplements come with Vitamin D in them, as well.[39]

Magnesium also plays a part in strengthening our bones as we age, as it converts Vitamin D into the active form that the body can use.[40] Magnesium levels also wane during the menopausal years, so we need to ensure we get enough in our diets or through supplements. Magnesium can help reduce the annoying symptoms of menopause such as insomnia, mood swings, anxiety, irritability, and water retention while improving energy levels, which tend to decrease. Women over 30 need to take in 320 milligrams of magnesium per day.[41] There are many foods that provide this nutrient naturally, including brown rice, spinach, lentils, oatmeal, kidney beans, bananas, and chocolate – yes, that's right, *chocolate!*

After hearing about the woes of fat for years, these days we are hearing praises of omega-3 fatty acids. With these mixed messages, it's no wonder we are confused about why and how these fats are good for us. Some studies show that omega-3 fatty acids may help increase calcium levels and improve bone density.[42] The *Journal of Clinical Psychiatry* also credits omega-3 supplements with being helpful in fending off depression[43], another symptom that can coincide with the menopausal and post-menopausal years. The anti-inflammatory properties of omega-3 fatty acids are of added benefit to menopausal women for heart, breast, and bone health. Studies have shown that omega-3 fatty acids may help lower the risk of chronic diseases – namely, heart disease, cancer, and arthritis.[44] Sources include wild salmon, flaxseed, eggs, canola oil, pumpkin seeds, and walnuts. A

---

[39] http://nof.org/calcium#howmuchvitamind

[40] Yeager, D. 2014, *Magnesium's Relationship to Bone Health*, Today's Dietician, Vol. 16, No. 12 P. 50

[41] https://ods.od.nih.gov/factsheets/Magnesium-HealthProfessional/#h2

[42] Ehrlich, S.D., Reviewed 2015, umm.edu/health/altmed/supplement/omega3-fatty-acids

[43] https://www.sciencedaily.com/releases/2010/06/100621111238.htm

[44] http://umm.edu/health/medical/altmed/supplement/omega3-fatty-acids

doctor may prescribe 1,000-3,000 mg per day for women with the health conditions omega-3 are proven to support.[45]

Now that we have been reminded of the benefits of healthy whole foods and the potential need for nutritional supplements based on our dietary habits, let's talk about the other factor in the healthy lifestyle equation: exercise!

All the Right Moves

It is a myth that as we age our metabolism (the process of converting food into energy) slows down. This only seems to be the case because our metabolism is intricately tied to energy expenditure. Realistically, most of us are a lot less active and expend less energy as we age. This leads to a reduction of lean body mass and an increase in fat storage. This starts to happen in our 30s; and no matter what we do from a dietary perspective, if we do not exercise, we can only accomplish a portion of the goal of maintaining a healthy lifestyle.

I find most women have a love-hate relationship with exercise. Just hearing the word is daunting for some, perhaps because we immediately think of lifting heavy weights, doing more sit-ups than our bodies are ready for, sweating, being ogled by men, and stinky gyms. For most of us, there is nothing sexy or pleasurable about these images. So let's lose those images and come up with some new visuals for getting more active.

It is commonly said that we need 30 minutes of physical exercise each day just to maintain our current weight. I don't know about you, but I have enough chores in my life – I need a fun way to get those 30 minutes in.

According to the Centers for Disease Control and Prevention, I am not the only Goddess not getting the prescribed 150 hours per week as the minimum exercise requirement needed to maintain a healthy

---

[45] https://www.womentowomen.com/inflammation/balancing-your-omega-3-fatty-acids-essential-for-health-and-long-life/

lifestyle.[46] 80% of American residents[47] and 86% of Canadian women[48] reportedly do not get the daily minimum exercise requirement. A related study found that inactivity is linked to one out of every ten deaths, totaling a whopping 5.3 million deaths worldwide. Therefore, our activity level is definitely something we need to pay attention to for healthy aging.[49]

As we age, muscle loss is inevitable, and our increasingly sedentary lifestyle speeds this up; so some strength training should be part of our 30 minutes of exercise each day, to combat this loss. Furthermore, scientists have predicted that women over 40 lose about 1% of their balance each year, so incorporating movements that support us in our mobility and flexibility will help prevent falls – another major issue for women as they age.

As mentioned earlier, women are more susceptible to feeling depressed as they approach menopause. The fact that exercise is mood-enhancing is just one more reason to get active. So grab a pair of 3-5-pound dumbbells, or simply start with two water bottles, and let's look at adding some movement to our lives.

 And NO, you can't drink the water first to make the bottles lighter!

Another option for those who are gym-averse (or simply don't have this option) is to start walking. It's something we all know how to do and it barely takes any energy, yet most of us don't do it. If you have been sedentary for a long time, I challenge you right here, right now, to go for a short walk today (provided your doctor supports you

---

46 www.cdc.gov/physicalactivity/basics/adults/index.htm
47 http://www.cbsnews.com/news/cdc-80-percent-of-american-adults-dont-get-recommended-exercise/ Note the US stat is all residents
48 http://www.thestar.com/life/health_wellness/nutrition/2011/01/19/only_15_of_canadians_meet_minimum_exercise_standard_statscan.html Note the Canadian stat is just for women
49 http://www.thelancet.com/journals/lancet/article/PIIS0140-6736%2812%2961031-9/abstract

in this) – even if it is to the end of your driveway and back. Make an effort. Build up to a five-minute walk and then add five minutes on the next day, and so on. For those of you not in this long-term sedentary category but needing a bit of encouragement to get started again, consider this your moment to get back into the routine. Why not start with a 15-minute walk today?

The year I turned 50, I had more aches and pains than a 100-year-old woman. I was told I would need surgery on both knees, I had lower back pain, and bending over was a chore. Although I was uncomfortable, I knew I needed to get in better shape. So, I started out on a treadmill and simply walked for 15 minutes each day. My reward (because I deserved one) was reading a novel while walking. I later substituted the novel with music, as that motivated me further. The daily exercise and increased stamina prompted some other lifestyle changes. I made healthier food choices, drank more water, and reduced my red wine consumption. In time, I progressed to a 40-50-minute walk-run routine. In 12 weeks, I lost 30 pounds and had no further issues with my back or knees. I felt great, both mentally and physically.

Reading Charles Duhigg's famous book *The Power of Habit*[50], I learned that changing a keystone habit (for me, this was changing from not doing any exercise to walking on a treadmill) triggers a domino effect, affecting other habits (healthier food choices, decreased food and wine consumption) as well. The changes I made were widespread and positive, and it all started with that first walk. By making single, small changes to support our transformation, we begin to see that greater achievements are within our grasp, which we automatically act upon.

As another example, at the time of writing this book, my mom has reached her lucky sevens.

---

[50] Available on the Transforming Venus website: http://transformingvenus. com/product-category/books/

No, I do not mean she won the blazing sevens on a slot machine at the casino.

I mean she has reached her 77th year as a Goddess. She has always loved to travel. A few trips on her bucket list were heaps more aggressive than the previous ones she had taken as a senior. One such dream trip was to the Galapagos Islands of Ecuador. To participate fully in a trip like this, she had to be physically able to leave the cruise ship by getting into and out of an inflatable boat in order to go to shore and see the fabulous wildlife of the islands. But that wasn't all; these Island walks require trekking over mostly uneven terrain.

My mom suffers from chronic obstructive pulmonary disease (COPD) and is on oxygen 24 X 7 and therefore was not in shape to take on this challenging adventure. My older sister suggested she get a personal trainer, and my mom agreed. She worked with the trainer to prepare for this trip over a four-month period. Then, with her oxygen in tow, she knocked the Galapagos Islands trip off her bucket list. Although she has traveled to many places in this wide world, covering five of the seven continents, this was her trip of a lifetime – so far! So if my 77-year-old mom with COPD could get a personal trainer and begin to work out (for the first time in her life, I might add) so that she could attain her dreams, what excuse can the rest of us possibly have not to get more active to attain our own goals?

 Don't put your dreams in the f*ckit bucket; take action by putting your body in motion and prepare yourself to meet them head on!

Thankfully, physical activity need not be strenuous to be effective. Nowadays, there is no shortage of fun and accessible opportunities to get moving. For example, do you like to dance? Zumba is basically exercise to music – they call it "exercise in disguise!" It's a fun way to get more active and shake your booty. I have done quite a number of Zumba classes in a lot of different places and I have come to the conclusion that if you do get lost in the moves, you can do your own thing. Coordinated movement is not my strong point, but Zumba is forgiving in this regard, not to mention so upbeat and fun it's easy to forget to be self-conscious! I always feel amazing after a Zumba class.

 So, even if you too have two left feet – do not fear, Zumba is here!

What's most important is that you do what you love, especially if you are rekindling your love affair with exercise. Take a belly dancing class, or ballroom dancing. Try kayaking, hiking in the woods, swimming or anything else that builds your energy reserves. And remember you can always build extra exercise into your day even more easily by seeking out opportunities to walk a little more. Live in an apartment building? Take the stairs instead of the elevator.

 Of course, if you live on the 30th floor you might want to rethink that idea!

Even if you do errands with a car, you can always park it a little further away than you normally would, and enjoy a few extra minutes of exercise. Or do you have a dog? There's nothing like a dog to get you motivated for a walk!

Keeping the home clean is always a great way to keep moving; and of course, yard work and gardening are also enjoyable ways to stay active and take in a little vitamin D.

Another great exercise option, particularly for the aging Goddess, is Tai Chi. This gentle yet powerful ancient system of movement is calming, meditative, and good for boosting brainpower and flexibility. Even better, no special equipment is required.

If you want to try something new, or have enjoyed doing a particular activity in the past, take it on! If you have been letting negative thoughts talk you out of things you think you should do or things you want to do, I hereby throw down the gauntlet and challenge you to a duel with your own little *itty bitty shitty committee,* that part of your mind that talks you out of doing things you know darn well are good for you. You need to shut it down. If *gauntlet* sounds warrior-like, it was meant to. It's time to go to battle with those negative thoughts that are not in your best interest. You inherently know what is good for you, and negativity does not win here!

This chapter covered nutritional and physical goals to support optimum health. The exercises that follow will guide you in documenting your planned changes to support your health goals.

 ## Exercise: Healthy Nutritional Transformation

Take a few moments to document three or four nutritional changes you plan to make right away or in the near future, to improve your eating habits. They can be based on the suggestions provided within this chapter or something else entirely. They may also include having a chat with your physician or health care provider about the potential need to add dietary supplements to support your nutritional requirements.

Respond to the following statements in the space below.

I plan to improve my health by taking the following nutritional action steps:

_____

_____

_____

1. My start date for nutritional action step one is: _____

_____

_____

_____

2. My start date for nutritional action step two is: _____

_____

_____

_____

3. My start date for nutritional action step three is: _____

_____

_____

_____

4. My start date for nutritional action step four is: _____

_____

_____

_____

Exercise: "All the Right Moves" Transformation

Now take a few moments to document at least one or two new movement changes you plan to make right away or in the near future. Again, they can be based on any of the suggestions in this chapter or something else entirely. Respond to the following statements in the space below.

1. I plan to improve my health by taking the following new movement action step:

_____

_____

My start date for this action step is: _____

2. I plan to improve my health by taking the following new movement action step:

_____

_____

My start date for this action step is: _____

Positive Affirmations Related to Health and Wellness:

- I have a strong, healthy body.
- I nourish my body with healthy foods.
- I feel energized when I exercise.
- New balance is coming to my body now.

Section III

Adventuring with the
Goddess Within
(Letting Her out to Play)

Chapter 13

Living True to Your Goddess Core Values

"Your goals and the tasks you choose to accomplish your goals either align with dream and core values or they don't. It's that simple." *Julie Connor*

Goddess Tenet #9: A Goddess lives her life authentically, portraying the same façade to the external world as she holds close to her heart.

Goddess Ellie, age 38, from Georgia, United States tells her story:

It's 3 a.m. and I'm exhausted. I've been in the office for 20 hours straight, running my team's annual general meetings. Our remotely operated international staff is spending a week in the UK, planning next year's projects.

My weary interns and producers are leaving the office with glazed eyes. We have half a week more to go, and everyone is ready to collapse. We need sleep, fun, and some time to wander the charming cobblestone streets around us to find inspiration again. I'm following my team out the door when the boss waves me into his office.

"I have some new ideas," he says. "We're going to add them to the production calendar." He means the one that got voted yesterday, before he re-wrote the minutes since he didn't like the vote.

I'm five time zones from home and I can't figure out why I'm still jetlagged after four days. I'm starving because we worked through dinner and didn't stop to eat. At this point, it's all I can do to respond in full sentences.

And one minor detail nobody else knows yet? Yesterday before dawn, two little blue lines stared back at me from a little white stick. I feel nauseated, but I can't tell if it's from pregnancy or jetlag and hunger.

My boss isn't even talking about his plans to triple the production schedule. I already know he doesn't care that the project plans were voted. He'll mix it around without regard for logic or productivity. Instead, he's talking about how some of the young female team members should take wardrobe lessons from his fashionable, sexy daughter. Next, he's daydreaming about exotic vacation plans with his wife.

I catch myself staring at the doorway, wondering why this can't wait a mere four hours until 7 a.m. when I'm back at my desk.

My boss is an extreme narcissist, and I'm realizing that I've been enabling his toxic behavior for years. I've been so busy pandering to his ego, managing his paranoia, and offering myself as a buffer to protect my team from his toxicity that I can't even pinpoint where my own life went off track.

He's the epitome of a man displaying different personae to different people. When speaking to large crowds around the world, he pontificates ivory tower theories on how to engage in meaningful relationships with people. Off the stage, he rules his support team with an iron dictatorship, keeping us constantly off balance and groveling to please his unpredictable whims.

He is a fraud. He has no single set of over-arching core values that define his identity across all environments. He cannot be trusted to do what is right or to keep his word, and the entire team knows it. I've stayed this many years because I believe passionately in the work we do, and because I thought I could somehow make it better.

I don't have a clue how or when I let my work life spiral so badly out of control. All I know is I want my innocence back. I want to live in the sunlight again, where I'm free to be transparent and straightforward instead of always glancing over my shoulder.

As leaders, we have two options: 1) keep our public and private faces separate and hope no one unmasks our fractured existence, or 2) shed the mask, own our values, and lead wisely.

I don't mean leaders shouldn't have private lives. As a business owner, social leader, mentor, and parent, I freely acknowledge great value in keeping one's personal life personal. I'm talking about being the same core person no matter the environment – home, work, play, travel. I'm talking about embracing those core values within every facet of leadership – not based on who we wish people would think we are, and not based on the expectations of whichever social circle we may be in at the moment. Private and public interactions must be driven by an identical set of values. Otherwise, at least one of our faces is a lie.

A few months after that pivotal night, I attended a workshop about discovering core values. I stared at lists of different possible values, and participated in guided exercises that helped me discover and articulate which five I simply couldn't live without. It was grueling, but it was worth it. By the end of the day, I had defined with certainty which things in life mattered most to me, and which values transcended the nice-to-have into the non-negotiable. For me, those crucial values are Loyalty, Excellence, Justice, Integrity, and Transparency.

Without these, I become frustrated, unfulfilled, and unfocused. The projects that make me come alive tend to center around building trust, bringing justice, and developing excellence. In contrast, pursuits outside my sphere of values make me feel reduced to just another cog in someone else's machine – which, I might add, is a feeling I really hate.

Knowing my core values ultimately brought me the freedom to say,

"Yes!" to amazing opportunities – and the freedom to say, "No," and walk away from that job. The resulting sense of confidence in who I am and where I want my life to go has been priceless.

∗ ∗ ∗

Earlier when we discussed mindset, I highlighted the importance of paying close attention to our beliefs and thoughts because of the vital role they play in our lives – especially in our ability to move forward to live the life we desire. Our beliefs are the start of our journey toward our destiny. A quote from Mahatma Ghandi walks us through this continuum: *"Your beliefs become your thoughts. Your thoughts become your words. Your words become your actions. Your actions become your habits. Your habits become your values. Your values become your destiny."*

 Stop and think about the truth of this for a moment. Consider the first part of this quotation: "Your beliefs become your thoughts." If we do not believe we can do something and we barely give it a second thought, guess where it will show up in our destiny. You're right: nowhere! The only place it might show up is in the *regret* category – regret at having listened to some limiting belief or the itty bitty shitty committee that robbed us of the chance to give it a shot.

Why Are Core Values Important?

Since this is a toolkit and guide to assist us in moving from drudgery to destiny, away from the hum-drum and uninspired and toward living our lives with purpose, it is important to pay attention to the last part of Ghandi's quote – *your values become your destiny!* The majority of us have given our values very little, if any, conscious thought in the past. We may have some idea of what they are, but have we stopped to define them fully? Or have we never been taught the importance of this? If our core values truly are our essence and destiny fulfillers, it's time to put some attention into defining our unique core values for this time in our life.

Whether or not we are consciously aware of them, all of us have core values that reflect what is most important to us. Core personal values are qualities or traits that represent our highest priorities and our most deeply held beliefs based on what we perceive as truths in life.

Our core values are revealed through our everyday actions and inactions. The clearer we are on our values, the more authenticity we bring to our choices. Once we have clarity on our core values, we are more able to use them as the beacon to help keep us on track. The more our values become embedded into everything we do, the more we are apt to stay in alignment with them and, consequently, on the right path to reach our desired purpose and our ultimate destiny. Are you aware of your core values, or even the importance of defining them?

 Our personal core values play a major role in supporting our dreams, vision, and purpose in life.

Our values are unique to each of us. You could think of them as guiding principles because they form a map of sorts, which defines:

- Who we are
- What we believe
- How we live our lives
- The person we want to be

They have a role in defining how we feel about ourselves, how we feel about others, and how others perceive us. Consider this: if one of your core values happens to be family and your boss insisted you work overtime one evening, causing you to miss an important family occasion, you would feel bad and perhaps somewhat violated because you had to do something that was incongruent with your values.

If integrity is one of our core values and someone we know does something that is dishonest, we would adjust our previous perception of them because their behavior is incongruent with something important to us.

Our personal core values go a long way in defining who we are as people. They are therefore a highly valuable component of our entire being. So where did we get them from?

Where Do Our Core Values Come From?

Our values develop when we are young, based on our interpretations of the interactions we have with our environment and the people within it. Examples include our parents, siblings, relatives, friends, others in society, our religious affiliations, social encounters, the media (TV, radio, newspapers), books we read, our teachers, and the list goes on. Once defined, our values impact every aspect of our lives.

As we grow, our values shift and grow along with us. We are always developing new values based on what is important to us at the varying stages of our lives. And some of us continue to hang onto old values that are no longer relevant. As life brings us new twists and turns, our core values need to be regularly refreshed, to ensure authentic alignment.

 Just like lipstick, you need to ensure the shade (core value) is still a great match for your new and improved Goddess self, the one who is now making a concerted effort to nurture herself!

 When things feel a bit off-track, it's a good time to investigate the congruency between your core values and your life.

Our values may have changed since we last paid attention to them, or perhaps we have never really given them much conscious thought. Either way, our current transformation through awakening, nurturing, and adventuring with our inner Goddess means the time to identify and clarify them is NOW. As a mature Goddess, we have thrown out some disempowering beliefs and, as a result, it's time to adjust our values compass.

Research has shown that as women, we define our values more clearly in midlife. Perhaps this is because we define success in different ways throughout our lives; or perhaps at this midlife crossroads, our goals and values are up for inner debate. Alternately, a dramatic or traumatic event has forced us to reassess our values; or perhaps it is just our internal clock subtly reminding us that time is ticking and we need to get moving if we want to accomplish our dreams in life …

 … such as living our Goddess life's purpose!

When I look back, I can think of several moments in my life when I was not in a growth mindset. Goddess hindsight has allowed me to realize that my response to the challenges I faced in those instances was incongruent with my core values, one of which has always been personal growth. I was out of sync and not living my life at my optimum level of integrity. Thank goodness I had a wakeup call, because living my life with meaning and purpose cannot happen if I am not in balance with my values.

I had been teaching college for almost nine years. While I loved it, things had settled into a routine and I missed the passion of creating something new like when I had first developed the program years earlier. I needed to keep learning, and I felt a strong pull to be an entrepreneur. My soul needed to create something new again. My quest of helping women, and my sense of adventure, led me to hand in my notice on my full-time professorship and role as program coordinator. Replacing the two-hour Monday to Friday commute to the college with a new four-day week working from home gave me extra time to adventure into entrepreneurship on a part-time basis. I now feel closer to living my life with purpose, and I am thoroughly enjoying the adventure. Knowing my values was a key factor in my decision to make the change. In the words of Roy Disney, "It's not hard to make decisions when you know what your values are."

A good way to use your core values in times of important decision-making is to pause if there is any confusion or conflict around the decision. Ask yourself if your choice is in line with what's most important to you in life at this point in time. If the answer is yes, you will be on the right track to creating congruency between your values and decisions, and more likely to make a positive decision moving forward. You can always return to your core values when you need inspiration and clarity, or re-evaluate a previous decision you are waffling on.

Values are powerful little gifts from the Universe. They motivate us and drive us forward to attaining what we want. Despite learning about values in business while working as a manager, earlier in my career, I had not put much effort in connecting the potential of personal values to living my best life. Since this *a-ha* moment came to me, and by paying attention to and constantly refreshing my values, I have seen some remarkable progress in my life.

You may feel comfortable sharing your core values, as Sarah did; or you may feel they are personal and, other than putting them on your dream/vision board, you may wish to keep them to yourself. As this book is intended to be a toolkit and guide, I thought it might be helpful if I shared my own core values. You will also note that I have reflected on why each value is important to me. Later, in the exercise section, you will be invited to identify your five core values. You may also wish to reflect on your "why" for choosing each value. You will note some of mine expand into my business. This may not be the case for you. You may also choose to do this if you are in a similar situation of redefining yourself with a business in mind.

My current, newly refreshed, core values are as follows:

1. **Authentic Love** – I am genuinely concerned for my family, friends, and all human beings. People who know me would say I support people in a kind, caring fashion and that I am sensitive to their needs. I am patient, understanding and extremely accepting, nurturing, and welcoming, with love

for each and every person's uniqueness. I passionately want to make a difference in people's lives.

2. **Passion** – Everything I take on I do with extravagant enthusiasm and focused determination. When recently asking 25 friends to describe me using only three adjectives, the majority of responses related to passion, determination, and being driven. Whether it's writing this book, taking on the new role of developing a new program as a brand new college professor, or developing my Transforming Venus business to support women who need me, I put my heart and soul into all my endeavors.

3. **Integrity** – I am committed to keeping my word in both personal and business dealings. In my personal life I maintain a high level of honesty, and people can trust what I say as true. In my business I strive to under-promise and over-deliver, and I always treat integrity as the only option – because my morality meter is always "right" on. *Pun intended!*

4. **Personal Growth** – I am and have always been a lifelong learner, and have spent a considerable portion of my life encouraging the personal growth of others. In fact, this is in my vision statement. Every day I work toward positive change in myself and strive to be the best person I can be. I live true to my personal AIM model: I am *aware* of opportunities for growth, I make an *intention* to act on this opportunity, and I *move* on this opportunity to further support my personal growth.

5. **Spirituality** – This is one of my newly refreshed core values that have evolved as I have become a midlife Goddess. Previously, as a mom raising three sons, family was a separate value. Of course, family is still critically important to me, but as my family have grown and moved into their own homes and lives, now is the time for *me*. My family have been encapsulated into my authentic love value. I have entered a time in my life where my spiritual curiosity, creativity, and sense of adventure are of keen importance. I am focusing on

reconnecting with myself and making a conscious effort to appreciate the beauty and adventure of life, and in living the best life I can.

These are the values closest to my heart right now. Here is an attempt at tying them together – a "values statement," if you will:

Because I am a passionate person who authentically loves and who believes in the power of personal growth – and as a person of integrity who knows better than to keep to herself gifts that will benefit others – I freely share my knowledge and wisdom with other spiritual beings, especially women, who are also on a path of curiosity and adventure with a desire to expand their own horizons!

How to Use Our Values in Our Life

It would be a real waste of time to go through the process of determining our core values and then just file them away as *faits accomplis.*

Completing the exercises in this chapter will serve us throughout our life if we remain conscious of our current core values and allow ourselves to be guided by them. They serve as a set of over-arching principles that will support us in consistent decision-making and taking goal-oriented action steps, based on what is most important to us at the time.

Self-Reflection Exercise: Identifying Your Core Personal Values

Use the following step-by-step process to identify your core personal values. For the first 3 steps, consider the questions in the context of both your personal and career life experiences.

1. A good place to start is by reflecting on a time when you felt really happy and confident in the choices you were making. During these times, what were you doing? Who else was part of these feel-good experiences? Other than these people, what else contributed to your happiness?

   _____

   _____

   _____

   _____

   _____

   _____

2. Now let's consider the moments in your life when you were the most proud. What made you proud? Who else was part of these prideful experiences? Other than these people, what else contributed to these feelings of pride?

   _____

   _____

   _____

   _____

   _____

   _____

3. Finally, let's reflect on the times when you were the most fulfilled and satisfied with your life. What needs or desires were fulfilled? How and why do you think these experiences gave your life meaning? Document any other variables that contributed to these feelings of fulfillment and satisfaction.

   _____

   _____

   _____

   _____

   _____

   _____

   _____

4. Why do you feel each experience you discussed was truly important and memorable?

---

5. Using this preliminary reflection work as a starting point, go through the list of values below. As you review each of them, put a checkmark beside the ones you feel are important to you. Focus on selecting all the ones you feel good about or that you care about. And don't worry about selecting "right" or "wrong" values, because there can be no right or wrong ones; they are always right if they matter to you.

Energy	Abundance	Accuracy	Cheerfulness
Affluence	Professionalism	Success	Punctuality
Prosperity	Wisdom	Recognition	Status
Relaxation	Reflection	Security	Privacy
Promotion	Power	Recognition	Authority
Reputation	Diversity	Synergy	Teamwork
Respect	Spirituality	Solidarity	Responsibility
Motivation	Optimism	Money	Mindfulness
Organization	Passion	Peace	Intimacy
Intelligence	Perfection	Knowledge	Joy
Kindness	Justice	Impartiality	Humor
Health	Honesty	Guidance	Growth
Happiness	Grace	Gratitude	Sensuality
Truth	Sympathy	Vivacity	Wealth
Maturity	Wonder	Solitude	Imagination
Sharing	Altruism	Dignity	Commitment

Beauty	Balance	Belonging	Courage
Endurance	Control	Determination	Curiosity
Customer Service	Leadership	Poise	Achievement
Ambition	Inspiration	Appreciation	Giving
Inner Harmony	Perseverance	Philanthropy	Advancement
Faith	Pleasure	Excellence	Adventure
Making a difference	Fun	Accomplishment	Friendships
Problem-solving	Love	Generosity	Assertiveness
Thankfulness	Ethical Practice	Loyalty	Articulateness
Fitness	Excitement	Fairness	Fame
Independence	Integrity	Education	Influence
Freedom	Caring	Fidelity	Advancement
Financial security	Sensitivity	Self-compassion	Bravery
Expertise	Directness	Exploration	Enthusiasm
Logic	Entertainment	Effectiveness	Discovery
Longevity	Virtue	Self-respect	Contribution
Community	Trustworthiness	Arts	Understanding
Sincerity	Solidarity	Spontaneity	Duty
Thoughtfulness	Tranquility	Cooperation	Eco-awareness
Empathy	Dreaming	Consistency	Attractiveness
Cooperation	Family	Discretion	Confidence
Belonging	Encouragement	Discipline	
Service to others	Concern for others	_____	_____

6. Next, look over and review the list of values you have checked, and spend some time narrowing these down to the top 20 values you feel matter to you most. Circle these 20. You may want to use a pencil, so you can edit or change your list as necessary.

7. Now, narrow down your top 20 values to the 8 that are most important to you. Write these values on the Top 8 Values list below.

Top 8 Values – These values matter, but sometimes it depends upon who you're with or what you're doing. Think about WHY your values can sometimes change, matter more, or matter less!

1. _____
2. _____
3. _____
4. _____
5. _____
6. _____
7. _____
8. _____

8. Next (and this may take some serious thought and reflection), narrow these down to your five most important values.

Always Valued – Your Top 5 Personal Core Values

1. _____
2. _____
3. _____
4. _____
5. _____

9. Now do some creative journaling/brainstorming with your five most important core personal values. Write down what each of these values means to you, personally.

Now that you have identified your top five personal core values, return to this list whenever you are making a decision. Ask yourself, "Is my decision in line with my five most important values?" If you are not true to these values, you will most likely find that you are not happy with the result/s of your choice(s) and decision(s).

How to Use Your Values to Make the Most of Your Life

Your core personal values, especially your top five, represent your deepest driving forces.

Respond to the following questions after you have completed these exercises:

Did any of your personal values surprise you? If yes, which ones?

_____

_____

_____

_____

As you look at your life today, is there congruency in what you say your values are and the structure, focus, and content of your current life?

Yes _____ No _____

If no, what changes do you need to make?

_____

_____

_____

_____

Commit to taking action on these changes and you will be on a better path, as congruency in life is not a luxury when it comes to core values; it is a necessity.

 Congratulations – watch for positive change as you make new life decisions with these core values in mind!

Positive Affirmations Related to Core Values:

- Following my core values provides purpose and meaning in my life.
- All of my thoughts, words, and actions affirm my core values.
- My inner and outer world mirrors my core values.
- Every affirmation I create supports my personal core values.

Chapter 14

Your Creativity Awaits

"When all is said and done, monotony may after all be the best condition for creation." *Margaret Sackville*

Goddess Tenet #4: A Goddess possesses imagination, passion, and enthusiasm; and these attributes shine through her very being, supporting her in creating her own destiny.

Goddess Rebecca, age 62, from Florida, United States tells her story:

Christmas was on the way and my hubby and I had committed to make our gifts for all of our grandchildren. I discovered not only a love for being creative but also the love that flows through using creativity to touch others.

Our ten-year-old granddaughter Mya wanted a bed for her American Girl doll; specifically, a bed she had picked out in the American Girl

Store. *Armed with a few pictures and some measurements, my hubby crafted a fantastic replica of the bed that was her heart's desire. Next, it was up to me to create the beaded curtains, canopy, and bedding. The goal was to match our princess' own bedding, which her other Nana and I had made. With fabric scraps in hand, I unsuccessfully attempted to purchase pre-strung 70s style beads. It became obvious that I was going to have to string the beads myself, so with days already full of activity, I found myself stringing beads and creating patterns in pink, black, and crystal late into the night.*

As I added beads, I thought of the beautiful little girl I love so very much and imagined the joy I hoped to see on her face. But I also found my thoughts turning to my own childhood, where there were no warm grandma memories. I couldn't remember ever receiving a single gift from either grandmother, both of whom were vague, unemotional, indifferent women. These memories were definitely not what I had anticipated when I'd taken on this project.

Over the next few weeks, as I worked intensely to create Mya's "perfect" gift, joy surged with each darling finished piece, but the negative memories kept coming. Tears flowed, and I saw the source of my own silent struggle with being a "good Grammy" to the six special blessings in my life.

I began to pray with each finished piece that my princess would feel a grandmother's love each time she looked at her gift. And with each finished piece, something happened to me – slowly, healing began to take the place of pain, along with a confident hope for my sweet grandchildren and the generations to follow. The old dysfunctional relationships had been cut off and a new legacy had begun. The gift was an outpouring of my love through creating, and that would now be passed on.

The healing that occurred in my heart that Christmas changed the dynamic of my family for generations to come, and became a stream that overflowed into the lives of others, as well.

Who knew that unleashing the creativity within us could be such a powerful agent of love and healing?

* * *

I have always believed that creativity charms the soul. Rebecca's story exemplifies this belief. Expressing our creativity opens the door to the inner world of our imagination. Our greatest gift is our imagination. Our creativity relies on it, and for many, our very soul relies on it. In my mind, creativity is defined as "the use of imagination to create something new." This *something new* may be intangible, such as an idea, a theory, or a new way of looking at the world; or something more concrete such as singing, dancing, cooking, baking, gardening, drawing a picture, coloring with a child, or writing a book of poetry. There are so many avenues for you to consider. The good news is: it's your choice. Creativity is a process *anyone* can implement.

Creativity is believed by many to be the essence of what makes us human. It is at the core of our ability to create the life – and ultimately the world – we want. Of course, there are a number of factors that derail us from fully exploring our creativity. Life is complex and full of distractions. I am not saying all distractions are bad – we just need to use them in moderation. Another factor that does not serve our ability to invest in our creativity is fatigue. If you think back to the last time you were really exhausted, you will understand what I mean. In this state, you have no energy to be creative. You are simply in survival mode.

 A tired, exhausted woman does not a creative Goddess make.

There is a growing body of knowledge that indicates the desire to contribute to the lives of others enhances creative thinking. It has been proven that when we open up to our creative selves, a powerful healing takes place that affects our entire being. Goddess Rebecca's story at the beginning of this chapter demonstrates this powerful healing effect.

Research has also proven that being engaged creatively has therapeutic benefits. It induces enhanced feelings of wellbeing, cognitive flexibility, and can improve our problem-solving capabilities.[51] Creativity through art, music, dance, and writing has the potential to serve as a healing balm for many health conditions, both physiological and psychological.[52] Overall, the amount of time spent being creative can have a direct positive impact on our health, happiness, and longevity.

 If creativity equates to health, happiness, and a longer life – I say bring it on!

Resurrecting an old, or exploring a new, creative outlet may be just the holistic prescription needed to invigorate and challenge that feeling of being restless and stuck. Imagine moving forward, feeling passionate about something that makes your heart smile, something that makes you hum a ditty of satisfaction about what you have created, or grin like the proverbial cat that found the cream. I hope you're thinking back to something from your past that provided even an inkling of these feelings, and that you have the desire to replicate these – or create something even better.

If you feel stuck on what creative activity you love to do, consider some of the options you have explored in the past and may have forgotten. Did you have a journal that you wrote in on a regular basis? Did you like to draw, or mold with clay? Did you like the challenge of untangling or fixing jewelry? Were you a sand castle master or a Picasso in the making? Did you sew, knit, or crochet? Did you arrange flowers, do decoupage or wood art? Did you like to play in the garden? Did you like to dance, play an instrument, bake, or cook as a young Goddess? Was there some other creative pastime that occupied your time and mind?

Resurrecting something from the past is not the only option. Perhaps there is a new creative outlet that your mature Goddess self would like to explore, such as helping others. We all need to feel we

---

[51] https://www.authentichappiness.sas.upenn.edu/learn/creativity

[52] Stuckey, H, Nobel, J. (2010), The Connection Between Art, Healing, and Public Health: A Review of Current Literature, American Journal of Public Health, 100 (2), P. 254-263

are serving others at some point in our lives. Maybe you are ready for an entrepreneurial adventure and the opportunity to explore your creative self to the fullest. I encourage you to get started. Or perhaps you have done this sort of thing all your life and it's time to help yourself now.

Creativity Is Ageless

We all use our imagination on a daily basis as we create new thoughts, new ideas, and new ways to solve problems. Remember the last time you laughed at what you once thought was a silly idea? That silly idea was your imagination creatively working its magic.

A growing body of research challenges previous misconceptions of creative potential being *just for the young.* In the past, it was thought that some people were creative and others were … not so much. We also know which bucket we would have put ourselves in, if asked to self-classify. However, new learning in the field of neuroscience has proven that creativity is not just for the chosen few. We *all* have within us the potential for creativity – and here's the bonus: age does not matter; creativity is ageless![53]

Our greatest opportunity to shine comes when we discover and explore our creative potential, which many of us do in our mature Goddess years. I think this suggests we are more willing to get out of our "comfort zones" as we mature, and therefore allow the natural creativity to flow unimpeded. And letting your natural creativity emerge as you get older is said to play a part in healthy aging.

Why is it that many of us only discover our creative potential when we are older? Perhaps this is due to being too busy being a friend and mother to all those who needed our help and guidance, combined with our roles in balancing countless chores, appointments, and a career, not to mention being CEO of the household at the same

---

[53] Sisgold, S. (2012). https://www.psychologytoday.com/blog/life-in-body/201210/creativity-is-ageless

time. Few of us had time to explore and discover our creative passion during those busy years – we were in survival mode! Now is a really good time to switch to growth mode and put some concentrated attention into something you really love and find fulfilling.

Passion and Creativity

One of the goals of this chapter is to help you rediscover your creative confidence and support you in finding the courage to try something new, or re-enact a previous creative endeavor you may have been passionate about in the past, with a renewed fervor. Passion and creativity are related, but they are not the same thing. When someone asks you to tell them about yourself, they want to hear what you are passionate about. Stated another way, passion tells them something about you and your interests. Creating is something you do as a result of your passion.

The good news is that both create energy. Passion and creativity complement one another. When you can connect the power of these complementary energy forces, you can utilize your skills and do whatever you desire to make a significant contribution to your life, your community, and the world.

 Isn't that a powerful thought?

Do you agree that when we were very young, we possessed unfettered creative expression? We would sing a song, not caring who was listening or what they thought of how well we carried a tune or even if we got the words right. We would draw with a wild passion and proudly show our masterpieces to everyone who happened to come onto our paths. We were delighted when our parents and caregivers attached our artwork to their fridges with magnets or tape. We would dance our way around the room and even in the streets, proudly expressing our joy or acting as some imaginary being. We would use every color in the crayon box and color both inside and outside the lines with reckless abandon, delighted with ourselves for creating such fine art. If we were lucky, others would lovingly support us in all our creative play.

Somewhere along the way, perhaps as we approached the awkward teenage years, things changed. During this phase of life, society had a major impact on our self-image and, in many cases, influenced us to become self-critical. Sadly, we became hyper-sensitive to how others perceived us, which had a significant impact on our behavior. We became beings who did not share freely and instead held back on our creativity, especially in public. For many of us, this time of our life represented the rapid demise of our creative flair. In many cases, the memories of the extreme scrutiny lingered into our adult lives, leaving us unwilling to return to our former creative self.

Once we got past those teen years and moved into our 20s and 30s, we might have had new opportunities to explore some of our previous creativity. Those of us with children – or even those who have had the opportunity to be around other people's children – may have seen this playful, creative side of our being emerge once again. We lost some of those creative inhibitions and sang, danced, colored, built, and created right alongside those precious children. When we moved into our own homes, we had the opportunity to decorate them – a creative experience of color, style, and individual choice. For many of us, this limited exposure has been the extent of our creative journey and we are at a point in our life where we realize we have a renewed desire to be creative again and the time to explore this component of ourselves.

By the time we reach the mature Goddess stage, we have gained much wisdom and realize life is meant to be lived to the fullest. The opinions of others, on which we once placed far too much emphasis, no longer bear much significance. This is perhaps the first time in our lives when we have the luxury of two precious commodities at once – both the time and money needed to devote to our creative endeavors. We may also be blessed with the joy of grandchildren, and have a keen desire to share with these precious little beings the creativity that abounds within the world and the people who inhabit it. We are open to the opportunity to reveal our playful, creative side once again.

Retraining Your Brain

This childlike creativity comes naturally for many of us. Exploring our creativity individually does not seem to be as simple. Even with all these positive factors seemingly supporting a perfect environment for furthering our creative exploration, fear of taking that first step is a common stumbling point in fully embracing our creative ideas. The best way to tackle this hurdle is to break down the challenge into small steps; and as we are successful with each step, begin to build creative confidence, incrementally. Not only will our confidence grow, the power of our limiting fears will weaken so that we can get past them and create the life we desire.

Scientific research has proven that something physiological happens within the brain when doing something really meaningful and important. It was once thought that the brain was an organ that grew only in childhood, and once brain function was lost, it was irretrievable.[54] Through the invention of brain-imaging technologies like magnetic resonance imaging (MRI), the ability to watch the brain in action has revealed new knowledge of the amazing ability of the brain to continue to change in structure and function well into old age.[55] This redesign functionality, known as neuroplasticity, allows our brain to rewire itself continually, based on our behavior and new learning. Our amazing brain, the most complex of all living structures, is constantly reorganizing and improving itself by transferring intellectual ability from one lobe to another, a process known as neural mapping.[56]

---

[54] www.articles/mercola.com/sites/articles/archive/2012/12/09/brain-plasticity.aspx

[55] www.mcgilldaily.com/2014/03/rewiring-your-brain/

[56] www.articles/mercola.com/sites/articles/archive/2012/12/09/brain-plasticity.aspx

For those of us with an interest in creating, this is great news because constant neural mapping means more connections between concepts and, therefore, more opportunity for creativity. When we learn the meaning of a new word, learn a new card game, or challenge ourselves with a new creative endeavor, our brain physically changes itself to adapt. Even better, this happens more often as we age; our brain is constantly cleaning house and reorganizing itself for optimal performance. Think of the brain as a complex road map and liken the neural pathways to roads. Consider being able to connect roads that currently do not connect and reroute the roads based on traffic and construction. Consider limitless possible connections. This is the beauty of neuroplasticity.

If we consider for a moment a visually impaired person, we can more easily grasp this concept. The brain rewires itself and opens up neural pathways to provide a heightened awareness within the other senses, such as enhanced hearing, in order to protect this person better.

In order to build a larger network of neural pathways, new learning and new experiences are worthwhile endeavors. We have all heard much about the value of training the brain through Word Search games and Sudoku puzzles. For example, it has been shown to slow age-related dementia. Incidentally, both meditation and physical exercise support the creation of new neurons, as well.

 You may not be able to teach an old dog new tricks, but thankfully you can teach a Goddesses brain new tricks!

Eight Tips to Support You in Your Creative Exploration

As stated many times in many different ways, in this chapter and in others, we cannot be passive participants in life and expect things to change. As with all development and growth opportunities, some action must be initiated. That's why I have come up with this list of ideas for how to get more creative in your life, right now.

1. **Start Somewhere**. Although you may have chosen several, pick one creative endeavor to get started on immediately, perhaps one you have already explored in the past.
2. **Carve out Time**. Life is busy – you need to set aside the time to explore your chosen creative activity. You may choose to do what I have done and get up an hour earlier to be creative. I use this time to write.
3. **Proceed Slowly or Full Speed Ahead**. Wade in slowly if there are things you need to purchase for your chosen outlet. The cost of some creative pursuits can add up, and you want to ensure you have chosen a good match prior to investing in supplies and equipment. If there is no cost involved with the creative endeavor you plan to undertake, the message is different: it's full speed ahead!
4. **Commit to Developing Yourself**. Fully devote yourself to developing your creative abilities. Set and document your goals, and set time aside each day to develop your skills. Even if you can only commit to 15-30 minutes a day, start somewhere.
5. **Develop a Morning Ritual**. Exercise creates energy. Creativity creates energy. Start your day with exercise and then spend some time on your creative endeavor. This tells your brain you're ready to create, and it gives you a great start before your "real day" even begins.
6. **Remove Your Distractions**. Find a space that supports your creativity needs but also provides you with a minimum of distractions. Turn off the notifications on your cell phone. Stay off the computer unless you need it for your creative work. Even then, focus on the work at hand and make a concerted effort to stay away from the various distracting social media and email functions. This is a lesson for me, too! I have carved out a space in my home to be creative, and it

is *not* in my home office with my main computer and all the distractions of email and Internet.

7. **Become an Expert**. One of the best ways to develop creativity is to become an expert in that area. Read, research, practice, and learn from others. By having a rich understanding of your topic or specialty, you will be better able to think of novel or innovative solutions to problems you encounter.

8. **Keep a Journal**. Document your creative progress in a journal. Later, you can look back at the progress you have made and you will be very proud of what you have accomplished. This spurs you on to challenge yourself even more.

 Constantly challenging yourself to do better and allowing yourself to explore the many new creative options out there keeps you inspired and allows you to grow and flourish.

Your Creative Outlet

Having a creative outlet is important. You may or may not yet know what your creative outlet is and how it might support your passion and purpose in life. Sometimes our creative ventures are hobbies and do not, for whatever reason, impact upon us uncovering our passions and purpose. They may simply be something we enjoy. Alternatively, our creative endeavors can be a major component of our passion and purpose. Regardless, they provide another opportunity to learn and grow.

If you're not yet sure what lights you up, the following exercise is designed to support you in unlocking the door to uncovering that creative something. For the purpose of the exercise, any activity you embrace with some semblance of interest and focus qualifies as creative. If you feel passionate about it – even better! Your mission is to pick choices that give you pleasure and satisfaction and in some way express a part of your unique being.

Exercise: Exploring the Goddess Creativity in You!

Tick all that you have had an inkling of interest in, or have enjoyed previously:

☐ Sewing	☐ Crocheting, Knitting	☐ Writing
☐ Blogging	☐ Drawing, Sketching	☐ Jewelry creation
☐ Selling	☐ Painting	☐ Short story writing
☐ Development	☐ Carving	☐ Energy work
☐ Journaling	☐ Organizing things	☐ Basket weaving
☐ Interviewing	☐ Cleaning	☐ Baking
☐ Cooking	☐ Collecting	☐ Antiques
☐ Pottery	☐ Stained glass	☐ Candy making
☐ Cake decorating	☐ Creating recipes	☐ Flower arranging
☐ Gardening	☐ Making people laugh	☐ Martial arts
☐ Yoga, Pilates	☐ Zumba	☐ Photography
☐ Song writing	☐ Playing an instrument	☐ Singing
☐ Acting	☐ Dancing (any kind)	☐ Bird-watching
☐ Reading	☐ Mentoring	☐ Scrapbooking
☐ Pinterest	☐ Social media	☐ Inspiring people
☐ Research	☐ Mall/Plaza shopping	☐ Internet shopping
☐ _____	☐ _____	☐ _____

Which three options are your absolute favorites?

1._____ 2._____ 3._____

If money were no obstacle, what new creative adventure(s) would you love to explore?

_____

_____

_____

What is it about this activity that piques your desire?

_____

_____

_____

Do you know anyone who is doing this activity from whom you could learn more? If so, list their name and contact information here. If not, spend some time learning a little more about this activity. Document your research in your journal so you have the information at hand to follow up.

_____

_____

_____

 ## Positive Affirmations Related to Creativity:

- My Goddess creativity is always in demand.
- I am a creative being consciously exploring new outlets for my creativity.
- Being creative is one of my great joys in life.
- Creative energy flows through me at all times.

Chapter 15

Exploring Your Passion(s)

"There is no greater gift you can give or receive than to honor your calling. It's why you were born and how you become most truly alive." *Oprah Winfrey*

Goddess Tenet #4: A Goddess possesses imagination, passion, and enthusiasm; and these attributes shine through her very being, supporting her in creating her own destiny.

Goddess Paula, age 56, from Ontario, Canada tells her story:

As you may recall from the introduction to this book, about five years ago and on the north side of 50, I recognized that I was feeling extremely restless in my life, just going through the motions. I was not in growth mode. When I did give it some thought, I was confused as to where my life was headed. I was stuck and didn't know what to do.

Somewhere along the way, I had disengaged from my creativity and passion. I felt my life lacked deeper meaning and purpose, and I knew I had to do a deep dive into myself to fix the situation.

As an avid student who has always recognized when I've needed some new learning, I immediately started on a personal growth path, to get to know myself. A new life journey began! I read every resource I could get my hands on, and began to practice many of the concepts I was reading about.

I attended a local group meeting, the intention of which was to support people wanting to make a difference in the world. I knew I was one of those people; I just didn't know how I was going to do that, yet.

The Law of Attraction, the universal law based on "like attracts like," was at work. A few weeks later, I heard a radio broadcast offering a free, three-day workshop for budding entrepreneurs. I signed up for it on the spot. This training program exceeded all my expectations, and I was absolutely convinced this was the critical moment of choice and opportunity for me. I needed a business coach! Through a somewhat intimidating interview process, where I had to share my newly percolating business ideas, inspired by the workshop content, I was delightedly chosen for the coaching program. The group who interviewed me were a somewhat daunting crowd, featuring many successful, high-profile people, including Oprah's significant other, Stedman Graham.

I then had to call my husband and discuss the significant cost of this opportunity. The first words from his mouth were, you guessed it, "So much for the free training!" The next words were much more inspiring, however: "Honey, I consider this an extension of your education. You have given everything you have attempted in the past your full attention, and I know you will do the same with this – go for it!"

The life-changing experience of exploring my passions began. My coach set me the task of re-evaluating my core values, and helped me nurture that budding business idea. To find my "why," I was also guided to read some powerful and inspiring books, some of which are highlighted in this book.

My "why," my passion to make a positive difference in the lives *of others, combined with a synergy of component parts (my personal core values, strengths, skills, and life experiences), led me to create a new business. Wealth of WOW was launched with me as the Chief Positivity Officer (CPO). Yes, I gave myself this title, but in some ways I earned it, as I am often referred to as Positive Paula.*

I set up a Facebook page with a target audience of women over 40. The postings for Wealth of WOW included messages that inspired a sense of awareness of the many WOW experiences in life, messages that empowered and educated – with a little bit of sass thrown in, to entertain. The feedback I received was all positive, with many messages of support. Some women told me certain messages were just what the proverbial doctor had ordered, meaning my timing was impeccable for what they were dealing with at the time. After building the Wealth of WOW Facebook page to 6,500+ fans over the next few years, I transitioned it to Transforming Venus to coordinate it with the brand I was building.

Through my heart-and-soul-searching adventures, and by taking action, I found my way out of being restless and stuck. I had been craving the autonomy, creativity, and freedom of being an entrepreneur and using this venue to feed my passion of making a difference in the lives of women living in the same sad place of undiscovered passion I had previously been.

In addition to the passion of entrepreneurship and making a difference in the lives of women, I have found other passions through this journey, including writing this book and getting to know myself – someone I had not paid much attention to in the past. My own inner Goddess has been awakened, nurtured, and is now living an amazing adventure.

Yes, life is an adventure – and a journey. You are now part of my journey and my adventure, and I am part of yours. My energy feeds your energy – and yours mine! It has always been this way. We are simply acknowledging it, now!

* * *

When discussing passion in this chapter, I am not referring to the negative thoughts some people conjure up of being reckless and self-involved.

 I'm also not referring to sexual love or desire. Sorry, ladies. This is not *that book!*

To ensure we are speaking the same language when discussing passion, let's consider a couple definitions from the Canadian Oxford Dictionary: "Strong enthusiasm" and "strong barely controllable emotion" both encompass the flavor of what I mean when I refer to passion. I am speaking about doing something you obsess over, something you absolutely love that brings forth powerful positive emotions.

 This visual might help. Think of a Labrador's deep obsession, its constant driving need to play fetch when a ball is nearby – that's passion!

Finding and doing something that is a natural fit for you represents your passion. Passion arises from the heart. When you follow your passions, you will love your life and feel fulfilled. When our passions are clear, we are better able to determine the goals to support them. Put another way, once we identify and focus on what fills us with passion, we will be infused with more positive emotions and an abundance of positive energy to go along with these feel-good emotions. Like a magnet, our passion pulls us to action. Passion is the driving force supporting us in achieving our goals and dreams; it provides the power to connect with our self and others, enabling us to reach our full potential and ultimately live our authentic purpose. In the words of Zig Ziglar, "Your passion is born when you catch a glimpse of your potential."

Picture water running naturally down a stream or riverbed. Imagine the energy it gains as it follows its natural path. Similarly, the energy of your passion builds as you align with your natural passion. When you do find your passion, you will have found that which lights up your core; you will know what you were made to do.

There is a strong correlation between following one's passion and feeling happiness. Living a life of passion has also been shown to reduce stress, strengthen self-confidence, and fuel our success. Talk about a win-win – it's time to put some effort into exploring what we are passionate about.

For many of us, the complexities of life have run us off-track. Add to this our pre-disposition to nurturing others and it's no wonder many of us haven't given enough time and thought to our own desires and what we are passionate about. As a result, we may not even know what our passion is.

Discovery is akin to adventure, and this chapter tasks us with a challenging exploratory adventure. But before we embark on this journey of exploring our passions, I ask the following question:

 "How big is your but?"

We all use the "yeah-but" argument to talk ourselves in and out of things – mostly out of things! We hold ourselves back because we are frightened of the unknown, or we have for one reason or another either forbidden ourselves to enjoy life or have forgotten how.

 I suggest we stop using the "F" words – frightened, forbidden, forgotten – and any other such negativisms holding us back.

It's time to venture off the island of "yeah-but," as it is ripe with unhealthy, poisonous fruit. Instead, let's venture to a new island: the Isle of Infinite Possibilities, where passion trees grow in abundance, and where we gain further clarity and shed a final layer of our previous debilitating condition – that of being restless and stuck!

 Have you heard the saying, "The buck stops here?" It means the responsibility for something is your own; you cannot pass it to another. Here's a new one for you – "The stuck stops here." The meaning is the same, but this saying also indicates a positive transformative outcome.

The famous playwright and poet T.S. Eliot once said, *"It is obvious that we can no more explain a passion to a person who has never experienced it than we can explain light to the blind."*

Think about the passionate people you know. How do you think they got that drive? Although I said the Isle of Infinite Possibilities is ripe with passion trees, these people you know did not simply pick their passions out of one of these trees. They had an interest in something and took action on it. They found what they were good at; and just like Zig Ziglar said, that glimpse of potential illuminated their passion. As they recognized their budding ability, they also found they liked doing it. They started to feel more confident and accomplished in it, bringing a newfound energy and love. They built up to the strong barely-controlled emotion called passion. They then felt the desire to work their buns off because of the feelings evoked by this powerful sensation. Then, their brain got into the gig, knowing they were onto something wonderful. Their heart knew that, like love, these feelings evoked by their passionate endeavors were something worth fighting for – and fight for them, they did!

In many ways, my Goddess story at the beginning of this chapter mirrored the steps I have outlined. I hope this story and chapter encourages you to start your own inner exploration, to look at your own circumstances and interests, to hone in on your unique passion. Join the passion revolution – the world needs more people who do what makes them come alive. The ripple effect that is created can change our world for the better.

The Benefits of Passion

Being passionate about something is what wakes us up in the morning before the alarm, with excitement to start the day and get at it. The day flies by as we are immersed in our projects, and we may even work into the evening. If we had to work these kinds of hours in our job, we would likely resent it after a while. However, when we are passionate about something, the hours and days fly by. Some people are blessed to have combined their passion with their job.

Combining our strengths and heartfelt desires is the perfect recipe for doing something in alignment with our life purpose. Everything starts to feel more positive. Our passion gains momentum and becomes contagious, igniting others to take action, too. Passion helps us through the hard times; it brings opportunity and opens the door to our success.

Now it's your turn. So let's get started!

Five Tips to Move from ~~This~~ to Bliss!

Fill in your own substitute for *This* – It could be: Stuck, Mediocrity, Simply Existing, Nothingness, Stagnancy, Unfulfilled, etc.

1. **Take a Time-Out:** Remember when you were a child and you were told to take a time-out? Usually it was because you were misbehaving. That is not at all what I am referring to here. Focus on the benefits of that time-out – a chance to look at things from another perspective, something our busy schedules do not allow – a time to reflect! This reflection often provides the necessary quiet time to tap into our inner self, resulting in the answers we are seeking. Journaling and meditation have been discussed frequently in this book as very useful resources for growth. Choose either the journaling or meditation option and either write or meditate freely about what you have done in your life that made you feel proud, happy, loved, gleefully consumed, or some other powerful emotion you had when you felt infinitely enthusiastic about something. When you are done with this exercise, spend a few minutes connecting the dots to see what picture presents itself.

2. **Feel the Fear and Do It Anyway:** A little courage goes a long way. We also tend to put things off by telling ourselves we'll *get to it* when we have more experience or time; but for the most part, we are just frightened and our excuses are masks we wear to avoid the fear. We need to face the fear, because it is only then that we can move forward in delving into our passions and, ultimately, achieving our purpose. Fear is another "F" word to stop using.

3. **Embrace Your Uniqueness:** We all have a purpose here on earth. We all have a combination of traits, talents, knowledge, strengths, skills, and creative talent. Yours are different from mine – we are all unique beings with something special to offer ourselves and the rest of humanity. We need to hone in on that something special and share the gifts that are uniquely our own. When you find your uniqueness, that is when you truly shine! It is not a mistake to love what you love.

4. **Sing a New Song:** We spin pretty fine tales at times, and sing from song sheets that are sad and, for the most part, self-limiting – stories and songs that relate to not being good enough, that minimize our value, that determine and minimize what we do and do not deserve, or that refer to and diminish our capabilities based on age, gender, and other poor unrealistic excuses. It is time to change the stories and sing some new songs – ones that praise our worth, ones with a chorus of confidence, and ones that take us a step closer to Passion Lane, where we uncover our passions and begin to fulfill the purpose we are destined for.

5. **Do What You Love:** It is so important to do what we love, especially at this juncture of our lives. Think about things that make you smile or even laugh right out loud. If the barriers you put in place were non-existent – time, money, experience, age, knowledge – what would you do?

Exploring Your Passions

This next section is intended to help you explore and solidify what your passions are.

Take a step back in your mind and revisit your childhood. Think back to long before you started a career and/or a family. Try to get a glimpse of what you loved to do when you were that young, precious child. What was important to you? What did you spend the most time doing? Was it dancing, building, collecting, drawing, nurturing, baking, playing music, playing sports, creating theatre, painting, writing, or something else? Do you still have that passion today, or did your passion balloon get popped, sending you on another path entirely? This is an ideal time to explore what you love to do. As you start to reflect, I encourage you to focus and not let disempowering beliefs drift into your mind space. They are dream and passion killers, just like any well-meaning dream and passion-popping busybodies from your past!

In her book *The Top Five Regrets of the Dying*, Bronnie Ware cites the number-one regret as, "I wish I'd had the courage to live a life true to myself, not the life others expected of me."

The internal glow that passion brings cannot possibly be held inside – it permeates our whole being. We need to find our own special something that brings out that powerful glow factor. Is it solving problems, healing, creating something, promoting peace, connecting with other human beings, being a trendsetter, or something else entirely?

Your passion does not have to result in something you can physically feel, such as a piece of artwork you have created. We are not all great artists like Michelangelo; nor are we all fabulous writers like Danielle Steel.

 Not yet, anyway – but we have the potential!

Self-Reflection Exercise: Exploring the Goddess Passion(s) in You!

As you respond to this exercise, think of passion as an intense emotional feeling and drive that feeds your soul. The options are not all inclusive, so feel free to add something new that better matches your energy triggers.

1. **Motivation passion.** Which of these *I love to* ... statements most motivate or deeply resonate with you? (Choose up to five)

   I love to ...

   ☐ Shop, collect, or obtain things.
   ☐ Get the highest quality for the best price.
   ☐ Conceptualize, picture, draw, paint, photograph, compose, or make renderings.
   ☐ Make something out of nothing. I enjoy getting something started from scratch.
   ☐ Have financial freedom. I want to be wealthy.
   ☐ Be the best. I enjoy setting and attaining high standards.
   ☐ Operate by policies and procedures. I enjoy meeting expectations.
   ☐ Make things better. I enjoy taking something already created and improving it.
   ☐ Convert people to my way of thinking. I enjoy shaping the attitudes of others.
   ☐ Lead the way, oversee and supervise. I enjoy determining how things will be done.
   ☐ Efficiently maintain something that is already organized.
   ☐ Bring order out of chaos. I enjoy organizing something that is already started.
   ☐ Be a servant leader. I enjoy leading others in achieving their goals.
   ☐ Create something from scratch.
   ☐ Be on stage and receive the attention of others. I enjoy being in the limelight.

- ☐ See things through to completion. I enjoy persisting at something until finished.
- ☐ Test and try out new concepts. I am not afraid to risk failure.
- ☐ Fight for what is right and oppose what is wrong. I enjoy overcoming injustice.
- ☐ Fix what is broken or change what is out of date.
- ☐ Assist others in their responsibilities. I enjoy helping others succeed.
- ☐ Make a difference in the lives of others. I enjoy helping others in need.
- ☐ Other _____
- ☐ Other _____
- ☐ Other _____

2. **People Passion.** Which people do you lean toward? (Choose up to five)

☐ Abuse Victims	☐ Homeless	☐ Unemployed
☐ Minorities	☐ Hospitalized	☐ Mental Health
☐ Women/Men	☐ International	☐ Gay/Lesbian
☐ Children	☐ Business Professionals	☐ Poor
☐ College Students	☐ Parents of Teens	☐ Single Parents
☐ Disabled	☐ Faith-Based Community	☐ Divorced
☐ Empty-Nesters	☐ Young Professionals	☐ Prisoners
☐ Underprivileged	☐ Stay-at-Home Moms	☐ Seniors
☐ At-Risk Individuals	☐ Teens	☐ Spiritual
☐ _____	☐ _____	☐ _____

3. **Issue Passion.** What issue(s) or concern(s) do you feel most strongly about? (Choose up to five)

☐ Aging	☐ Abortion Awareness	☐ Addictions
☐ Administration	☐ AIDS	☐ Arts

☐ Childcare ☐ Creative Projects ☐ Counseling
☐ Divorce Care ☐ Diversity ☐ Economic
☐ Family Issues ☐ Financial Issues ☐ Environment
☐ Health Care ☐ Sexual Orientation ☐ Housing
☐ Neighborhoods ☐ Community Outreach ☐ Injustice

☐ Human Rights ☐ Education System ☐ Literacy
☐ International Issues ☐ Interpersonal Relations ☐ Teaching
☐ Legal Issues ☐ Ministryinvolvement ☐ Parenting
☐ Physical Fitness ☐ Inspiring People ☐ Music
☐ Politics ☐ Poverty ☐ Racism
☐ Social Issues ☐ Teen Concerns ☐ Technology
☐ Mental Health ☐ Planned Parenthood ☐ Violence
☐ Terminal Illness ☐ Defending the Faith ☐ Hunger
☐ _____ ☐ _____

4. **Passion Summary.** Document your top five responses to questions 1-3 in the appropriate category below.

Motivation passion(s):

People passion(s):

Issue passion(s):

5. **Questions: Passion Indicators**

a. Based on your responses, and assuming time and money were not an issue and you knew you could not fail, what comes to mind as your passion(s)?

_____

_____

_____

_____

b. Considering your responses, what area would you love to look back on at the end of your life and know you had made a difference? Think of what you would want your own obituary to say about how you lived your life.

_____

_____

_____

_____

c. If your name were mentioned to a group of your friends, what would they say you were really interested in or passionate about? If you have children, what would they say about your passions?

_____

_____

_____

_____

d. What gets you excited and happy about life? What fires up your soul? What causes you to stay up late at night and get up early in the morning to do more of it?

_____

_____

_____

_____

e. What did you really enjoy doing as a young Goddess (a young girl)? What person did you want to become before life redirected or derailed you in a totally different direction?

_____

_____

_____

_____

f. Where do you (currently) anticipate spending your time, talents, and skills to help make your life what you want it to be?

_____

_____

_____

_____

6. **Passions.** As a final component for this passion exploration exercise, make a note of up to ten things you absolutely love. No, ice cream does not count. These should be things that relate to how you want to live your life, things that bring you joy, and things that would support your ideal life.

i.   _____

ii. _____

iii. _____

iv. _____

v.   _____

vi. _____

vii. _____

viii._____

ix. _____

x.   _____

The goal is to hone this list down to your top five passions. You absolutely can have them all, but finding the top five will help you see where to set initial goals to achieve this ideal life. You now need to go through this list again and add a feeling statement to each passion. Then review your list and, based on what you have documented on how each passion makes you feel, choose the top two or three that give you the most energy. Now, start putting some extra effort into ensuring they have a prominent part in your life.

See if you can identify your key potential energy/passion, and use it to write a passion/vision statement. Here are a few examples:

- I am a natural leader and lead others in achieving their goals (or in some other way).
- I live a life that has me being of service to large numbers of people.
- I help needy individuals in my community (or somewhere else in the world).

My Own Passion/Vision Statement is:

_____

_____

_____

Congratulations on honing in on your passions and writing a passion/vision statement that supports you in living your ideal life.

If you have still not narrowed down your passion, don't give up! It may take more than a few exercises to figure it out. Remember I am here to support you on your journey. You can send me an email to paula@transformingvenus for additional resources.

Positive Affirmations Related to Passion:

- Everything I do leads me straight to my passion.
- I am passionate about my path in life and pursue it with intensity.
- Living my life intentionally brings me passion.
- My passion about my life fills me with excitement and energy.

Chapter 16

Following Your Goddess Dreams

"The great courageous act that we must all do is to have the courage to step out of our history and past so that we can live our dreams." *Oprah Winfrey*

Goddess Tenet #10: A Goddess has learned balance, and strives to utilize her down time for both personal growth and adventure through play.

Goddess Tabatha, age 54, from British Columbia, Canada tells her story:

Belief in your dreams – knowing and feeling absolutely certain that something special, something you have always dreamed of, is coming your way – is a powerful thing. For me, creating that state of certainty to believe in and follow my dreams is crucial to making them come true, however difficult circumstances might seem at times.

One of my earliest dreams was to have a loving, healthy relationship that would last forever. Ever since I was a little girl, I dreamed of the fairytale – falling in love, having a couple of healthy, happy children, and living happily ever after …

I did get married – and yes, I have two beautiful, healthy children – but the "happily ever after" part did not last. My husband was a sex addict and after nine years of marriage, his addiction and infidelity finally became too much for me to bear.

My heart had been broken. But I was persistent. I knew there was someone else out there who would really love me the way I had always dreamed of being loved.

Being positive is the key, and I allowed my dream to be at the forefront of my life, no matter how rough things may have gotten at times. My dream gave me a sense of purpose and kept me motivated, inspired, and energized. I was not giving up; I would continue to pursue my dream. To the dreamer, nothing is impossible.

My attitude and mindset was important in my manifestation. I did not surrender to negative assumptions like, "I'm too old," or, "It's too late for me." I challenged them. Even through the hardest of times, I always reminded myself, "Where there's a will, there's a way."

I knew that great dreams take time to mature and blossom. When nothing seemed to be happening, I did not give up hope – ever!

Even as a single person, my life was very happy. I had a loving supportive family and wonderful friends. I had a great job, with delightful co-workers. Still, that feeling of something missing was always there and I needed to work out how to fill the gap. In my search for the man of my dreams, I signed up for multiple online dating services. After going on many – and I do mean many – dates, I learned to recognize the ones who were sincere and the ones who were not. This went on for a few years, and I even had a few long-term relationships, but these never grew in the way I hoped. I knew in my heart that there was someone else out there for me. I persevered. I continued to keep my dream alive to find "the one" for me.

Raising my children was one of my greatest achievements, but they were now grown and I knew I needed to direct my focus elsewhere. I knew my dream would manifest in the real world, but I needed to love myself first. In reading the book Law of Attraction *by Michael J. Losier, I learned to create the "good vibes" to help me "attract" what I was looking for.*

And then one day in May, it happened. It was the day my dream came true.

It was cold and rainy, and I was on yet another date with a man I had met online. But this one was different. Most guys want to meet at a coffee shop – romantic, right? But this gentleman – suggested we meet at the Oak Room Lounge in a historic, romantic, upscale premier five-star hotel. I saw him the moment I walked in, and meeting him felt special right off the bat. Shortly into our conversation, it was obvious we were "into" each other. The conversation flowed and we laughed and talked for hours. I didn't want the date to end, and I really wanted to see him again, so I boldly asked if he would be interested in joining me the next night for a friend's dinner party. He accepted, and I knew we were on our way.

Finally finding love was like two soul mates coming together. The world is a better place because of the love we share and the passion we generate. Our chemistry and shared vision of our life has always been undeniable.

Exactly six months later, in November of that same year, at the same Oak Room Lounge, that same man, now "my" man, got down on one knee and asked me to marry him. My dream really did come true and I have never been happier.

* * *

The statement "Follow Your Dreams" is a commonly recited inspirational statement – and rightly so. Our dreams have power! They pull us like a magnetic force into the future, and provide silent encouragement for us to move forward and accomplish our goals. In fact, it takes more energy to ignore an inner longing than it does to take a leap of faith to bring the dream closer to reality!

Life is a grand adventure of learning, growing, and dream attainment. Dreams keep us going, and we need to pay attention to them. Looking at Tabatha's story, her dream to find someone who would love her the way she deserved to be loved was always there in her mind. It promised happiness, fulfillment, and love. She did not give up and live a life without men; she continued to search for Mr. Right and her dream did not let her down.

You are a unique Goddess with unlimited potential. You may already know what your values, passions, goals, and dreams are. You may know precisely who you are and where you are going. If so, you are one of the lucky ones. For most of us, this is not the case; especially at this stage in our lives. We are different women now from who we were in the past. With the life changes we are undergoing at this mature Goddess stage, attaining our dreams and living a life of purpose is of paramount importance. Our dreams might need a slight refresh.

OK, a slight refresh sounds like a lipstick touch-up, which may be a colossal understatement. The need for an experienced makeup artist with a magic genie in tow might be a more accurate analogy of what is really needed – yes, a full "do-over"!

We need to nurture our dreams – we need to breathe life into them, to nourish them as they come to fruition. We need to clear our minds so we can hear the dreams our heart is whispering to us. Meditation, visualizations, and journaling are three examples of tools we can use to support clearing our minds. I encourage you to do some conscious dreaming here. You need to listen carefully so you can hear the dreams your intuition tells you are the most right for you at this juncture of your journey.

 Your dreams have the power to change your life.

Life throws us many curve balls. The bills sometimes seem to be higher than our income. Some of us have pitifully unfulfilling jobs. Marriages fall apart. Loved ones pass. Numerous other seemingly unsurpassable roadblocks get in our way. It's hard to consider our dreams when we feel we are simply in the throes of survival. However, the truth is our dreams are a powerful force that can help us get through even the worst days, providing the necessary impetus to keep going and change the status quo. We all have something special to give to this world. What's more, without taking action, we are not only neglecting *our* needs, but those of the greater good of all of humanity.

You might be thinking, "My dream does not affect others," but consider this: when you are living your dream, do you not think you will feel differently? You will operate at a higher energy level. Do you see how that higher vibration will impact others who come in contact with you and positively affect their lives, as well? That is the power of dreams – they invigorate us and those who around us. When we follow our dreams, others are inspired to do the same. In this way, the masses benefit from our dreams.

We have to overcome a lot of mental obstacles to take the first step to fulfill our dreams; but it is so important that we do so, as this kick-starts the whole process. We can't wait until the situation is perfect, because perfection is an illusion. Our situation may never be perfect. We simply need to take some small action and wade in. It does not matter if our skill and knowledge levels are not fully advanced to the level we think we need to reach to begin. We will learn more by *doing* than by waiting to learn all we think we need to learn. *Doing* is the fastest way to hone our skills. We also cannot wait for the approval of others – not everyone will agree with our ideas. Our dreams, or the steps we choose to get there, may well bring on some opposition from friends and family.

The message here is clear: don't wait. Take baby steps. Wade into the waters of your dreams, and allow yourself the benefit of growing with and through each dream as you attain it. You have always wanted to do this. You will experience things you never could have imagined, on your journey. You will become more courageous with each step. Your joy and happiness will be contagious, and you will be so proud of yourself and your accomplishments. The best time to start is right now!

You may need to come up with new dreams, if your previous ones are no longer relevant. Or perhaps your dream is a little foggy and needs clarity. The following exercise is designed to support you in dreaming a new dream; or alternately, blowing that light fog out of view and bringing that clarity of vision you so desperately desire.

Self-Reflection Exercise: Your Goddess Dreams

Each of the following reflections has multiple parts. Respond to all parts of each scenario or question in the spaces provided.

Consider this scenario: Yesterday you got to live your perfect first day of your future dream life. It is now the next day and you are passionately stating, "That was everything I thought it would be. It was my absolute perfect first day of living my dream; it's what I've always dreamed about!"

Describe everything about yesterday and your perfect day. Think of what you did and who you did it with, if anyone. Where did your perfect day take place? Describe the environment and the emotions you experienced as you did everything you wanted to do. What most excited you about the experience? Remember it was a perfect day – did it open your heart as you expected it would? Did it speak to you in an "I love my life" and "I deserve to live my dreams" capacity?

_____

_____

_____

_____

_____

_____

_____

_____

Considering your personal transformation, if you knew you could not fail, what dream would you breathe life into today? Would it be a mirror image of your yesterday as described above, or something else?

_____

_____

_____

_____

_____

_____

_____

_____

_____

Now that you have seriously considered and committed to paper your heart's desire, it's time to take action. Fully living your dreams is seldom possible in one fell swoop; most often you need to put some things in place to support them fully. If your dream is to travel to a different continent and the money is not readily available, you may want to get a book on your choice destination and start to plan what sites you would like to see there. You may also need to set up a travel fund and regularly deposit a portion of your income into this account. Any unexpected money, such as birthday money, an inheritance, casino winnings, rebate checks, etc. could also help fund this adventure. If your dream is to write a book, consider beginning by writing a guest blog for a blogger site, or commit to paper an outline of what chapters you would include and the working title. Once you have started to give this dream some focus by thinking about it and visualizing it, you will be well on your way to making it happen. When you visualize your dream, think about how you will feel when it is accomplished (e.g. happy, excited, proud, exhilarated, etc.).

 ## Exercise: Creating a Dream Board

A powerful tool many people find helpful for focusing their intentions and visioning their desires is a dream board, also known as a vision board. Before you start on your dream board, pop back into chapter 13 and review your top five core values, as these should be in the forefront of your mind as you do this work.

Remember – as Mike Dooley declares, "Thoughts become things." In other words, we bring about what we think about. By visualizing these desires, and by taking some action, the Universe conspires with us to make them a reality. This is the principle at work with a dream board – we are surrounding ourselves with these thoughts and dreams by putting them to paper and visualizing them daily. This visual cue motivates us to take action steps toward achieving our dreams. Imagine the life-changing opportunity here if our dreams are aligned with our life purpose.

If we consciously choose thoughts that portray what we truly desire in life to make us happy, and do not simply dream of having more material possessions, the Universe will help us move closer to the attainment of our dreams. This does not have to be some grand plan of saving the world; it is simply what we are meant to do by living in alignment with our core values and desires.

Anytime is a good time to create a dream board. Some women enjoy creating one fresh every year on New Year's Day, while some make dream boards whenever they are inspired. You can keep adding to yours over time, as more and more dreams come to mind. It's up to you how to use it once you've made it.

You may have very clear goals and dreams. In this case, you should create a dream board in the "I am clear and ready to manifest exactly what I want" style. Or maybe this is something very new to you and you are finally ready to discover what your dreams are. This is the second, more common "I am staying open to whatever the Universe has to offer me, based on my core values and known desires" variation on dream boards.

If you are in the "clear and ready to manifest" category, cut out pictures and images that match your known intentions, goals, dreams, and purpose. You are on a mission and know what you want. You should also use key words that support your vision; you likely already know what they are. Even if your vision is well-defined, a dream board is still very worthwhile to complete. You will have an easier time finding your images, especially if you have picked the right magazines. If you want an oceanfront condo, you would start with travel magazines. If you want a luxury yacht, you might start with yachting magazines. If you want to open a dog training facility and pet spa, you will want pet magazines, and so on.

If you are in the category of being "open to whatever the Universe has to offer," you are less certain about your intentions, goals, dreams, and purpose, or you have no idea yet, as you have not given yourself the time to consider this. What you *do* know is the importance of having a vision that is in alignment with your personal core values. If you skipped over the core values exercise, go back and complete it before beginning this creative work. As we say in education, it is a prerequisite, meaning this work builds on the core values work, so it must be done first.

If you are a "staying open" Goddess, you will approach this creative work from a different perspective from the "clear and ready" group, as you are still searching and staying open to whatever resonates with you in this creative journey and beyond. Cut out many more pictures of things that delight and interest you. Unlike the focused "clear and ready" group, your images will likely be from many different categories. This "staying open" vision board style can serve as a powerful guide, speaking to us and teaching us about ourselves and our passions as we go through the process.

Below are the steps to creating your dream board.

Step 1 – Prepare Your Supplies

1. A sheet of poster board, a few sheets of plain paper, and a picture of you.
2. Colored crayons, pencils, or markers.
3. Clear tape or a glue stick; scissors.
4. Assorted bling (sticky jewels) or scrapbooking stickers.
5. A list of inspirational words that really resonate with you.

6. An assortment of magazines and any pictures you have saved as desires (e.g. parenting, money, travel, design, wedding, retirement, shopping ideas, home, leisure, nature, pets, etc.).

You can also print pictures from the Internet that represent your desires, if you cannot find a picture in a magazine.

Step 2 – Prepare Your Mind

Mindset is key, and creating a ritual to support you will help put you in the right frame of mind: open and loving. We want to prepare our mind and cue our imagination to manifest thoughts on the life changes we truly desire.

1. Find a quiet place where you will not be interrupted for 10-20 minutes.
2. Sit quietly in a comfortable chair.
3. With loving kindness, and an open heart and mind, ask yourself what it is you want for the rest of your life.
4. Allow your mind to percolate and be with whatever images and words come to mind.
5. The preparation process makes for a deeper, more creative experience.
6. Put on your favorite music and your creativity hat, and start the next step of the project.

Step 3 – Prepare Your Dream Board

1. Go through the magazines and cut out any images that speak to you, based on what came up during your quiet time imaging. If nothing did, cut out pictures that resonate with you. If you cannot find a picture that resonates with your imagery, check on the Internet. Click on any images you like and then print them.

2. Using the crayons or colored pencils, write out words that resonate with you on the plain paper.

3. Place the pictures and words in a pile for now.

4. Place your favorite picture of yourself in the center of the poster board, or simply place your name in bold letters, if you prefer – perhaps in a heart-shaped cut-out that you have decorated using crayons and bling.

5. Sift through the pile of images and words and pick your favorites. Lay them out on the poster board in whatever way looks best. You can pick any of these styles or create your own unique display. There is no right or wrong way to do this.

Options

a. **Story Board:** Picture one thing happening, and then the next. Start with that picture of yourself in the top left and make a story board of all the things you would like to see in your future to support your dream. You might choose to organize the images from left to right, top to bottom, like a series of comic strips. Alternatively, you could arrange the images in a spiral pattern, starting with yourself in the middle and all the positive things you want to happen radiating outward from that picture.

b. **Themed Corner:** Health pictures and words are in one corner, relationship pictures and words are in another, career might be in a third corner, and lifestyle might be the forth corner. Another option is to have corners that focus on the statements, "I want to be ..." "I want to see ..." "I want to give ..." or "I want to have ..."

c. **Collage**: Pictures and words are randomly placed and they overlap each other. You likely did something like this in grade school. Remember part of our getting unstuck and living the life we really want means inviting our inner Goddess out to play. Do it; have fun with this. It's *your* dream board, so use your imagination and create whatever it is you are inspired to create.

Once you are happy with your display, use glue or tape to secure everything. Hang your dream board in a spot where you will see it often, and continue to manifest your desires through visualizing them on a regular basis. Remember: we bring about what we think about; and it only stands to reason that we will think about what we see, that much more often.

Another alternative to making a paper-based dream board is making it on the computer. Using word processing or slide show software, create a montage of pictures and words following the appropriate steps above, based on this electronic format style.

 ## Positive Affirmations Related to Following Your Dreams:

- All my dreams are coming true.
- Nothing can stop me from achieving my dreams.
- I dream my dreams, I believe my dreams, I receive my dreams.
- I can visualize my dreams coming true; I am grateful to the Universe for this.

Chapter 17

Goal-Setting with Intentions, for Goddesses

"Life best lived is life by design, not by accident."
Jim Rohn

Goddess Tenet #10: A Goddess has learned balance, and strives to utilize her down time for both personal growth and adventure through play.

Goddess Tracy, age 62, from Texas, United States tells her Goddess story:
April 30, a few decades ago
A beautiful spring day in Texas and I am enjoying a rare day off before starting a new job.
Just after 2 p.m., the phone rings – a familiar yet strained voice tells me my mother has just been killed.

That voice belonged to my father, the only witness to my mother's death at the hands of a drunk driver.

In the aftermath of this event I turned to MADD, Mothers against Drunk Driving, to try to make sense of this tragedy and to be with others who had similar experiences. I firmly placed myself on a path with one goal in mind: to end the heartbreak of impaired driving. I knew – I just knew – I alone could do it! I was so sure I would accomplish this goal. Attaining it consumed my every waking moment.

For the next ten years I lived in a dark place populated with others who hung onto grief, anger, and despair. Every time I heard another story about an alcohol-related crash resulting in death or injury, I would relive that April afternoon. As part of a restorative justice program, once a month I spoke before an audience of first-time "driving under the influence" (DUI) offenders, telling my story, sharing my pain, and ripping the bandage off my injuries in the hopes that just one of the people hearing me would make a different CHOICE in the future.

I did this month after month, over and over and over again, for ten years! I spoke before panels of judges and district attorneys. I even testified before a senate sentencing committee. I served as an advocate for others as they navigated the waters of the legal system. And when I felt exhausted, emotionally spent, I would remind myself of my goal …

One evening in 2007, I headed out, as I had each month to make the 30-minute drive to the courthouse to share my story. Halfway there, I knew with a certainty that rocked my soul that I could not do this anymore!

This "knowing" was so blinding I pulled off onto the side of the road, shaking, crying, scared … wondering what my life would be like without this monthly fix. Who would I be if I severed this connection to my past, to MADD? What would happen if I gave up on my goal?

As my sobs quieted, I took a few breathes, pulled back out onto the road, and drove on to the meeting – to tell my story for what I thought would be the last time, as both a victim and a survivor.

Days and then weeks passed, and I began to climb out of the dark. I read books, attended seminars, watched videos, and participated in webinars, all with the ultimate intention of figuring out how to create a new me, a new life, a new future.

Throughout all of this I never set any goals, yet there was at all times an underlying intention to get well, to heal, to become whole, to know myself again. The idea of setting goals made me tremble – because for me, not attaining a goal would be utter failure, and at that point on my journey I only knew failure to be bad, something to make you hang your head in shame. After all, I did not rid my world of alcohol-related crashes.

As I moved closer to living in the light, I realized my purpose had shifted. Somehow, someway, I wanted to share with others how to emerge from those dark spaces – to rediscover how to live in joy, to live in the light. Yet, I had no idea how that would happen, what it would look like.

I had been receiving Mike Dooley's daily Notes from the Universe for several years. In 2011, at the end of one of these notes was an invitation to take part in a program to become a certified trainer in Infinite Possibilities: The Art of Changing Your Life! There it was, on my computer screen, a possibility of what I could become: a trainer to bring a message of hope and empowerment to others! It felt as though the Universe knew what I was yearning for and had placed it right in front of me. How could I say no?

But I had to, as I was the primary care provider for my dad, who was moving toward transitioning from this life to his next. For a brief moment I grieved that "lost opportunity." Then, in the very next moment, I promised myself I would be at the next program. Oh please, I thought, let there be a next one, and let the timing be perfect!

As the Universe would have it, my dad transitioned the very week that first training was held ...

I kept the promise I had made to myself. In June 2012, I attended my first Infinite Possibilities: The Art of Changing Your Life training. I left that training confident in the audience I wanted to share this empowering knowledge with: women, women of any age in transition of any type. I felt my life experiences up to this point would allow them to relate/connect with me, and through this amazing program I could play a small role in guiding them to transform their lives.

Over the next several years, I tried just about every way I could think of to bring the message of this program to women. While I had some success, most of the time I felt like I was swimming upstream! I could not understand why women were not eagerly signing up for my workshops, engaging my services for one-to-one coaching, asking me to speak to women's groups! I had this potentially life-transforming information worth its weight in freedom, and yet there was resistance out there that I could not wrap my head around!

I could have given up at any point along this journey, but I **knew** in my very being that my intention came from my heart; that the principles laid out in this program had the potential to transform other lives, as it had mine! I kept moving, moving forward in small steps, expanding my knowledge base to include the latest research in neural science and epigenetics, the power of meditation. I knew all the answers we seek may be found within, that happiness is indeed an inside job!

Today, less than four years after attending my initial training, I am living the future I envisioned, without being attached to how it might come to be. Collaborating with other women, I have facilitated women's empowerment retreats; I have been a guest speaker at several events, with more to come, and a featured presenter at Infinite Possibilities Train the Trainer conferences; I have designed a women's empowerment program about creating amazing, sustainable change and living life more consciously, more deliberately, by becoming aware of our own unique and divine power!

One lesson I have learned along this journey is that for me, setting goals limits the possibilities, keeping us in a state of "old world thinking" – like the uprights on a football field or the net on a basketball court. These are "goals," clearly defined, with limitations.

Intentions have no borders, no clearly defined edges allowing for possibilities to show up that we could never imagine, to be in a state of "new world thinking." This is a state I much prefer; it is a state where we all can realize our fullest potential to be the next best expressions of ourselves!

* * *

Napoleon Hill, author of *Think and Grow Rich*, wrote about the habits of people he had studied for 20 years who had amassed personal fortunes. He then applied these principles to anyone choosing to achieve success in any area of life. One of these principles has to do with goal-setting. Almost every "success guru" has talked and often written about the art and practice of goal-setting. I've studied this myself and have found the practice to be extremely helpful in many areas of my life.

As I began to study spiritual principles, especially learning to "live in the now," I learned that spiritual teachers focus more on setting intentions than on setting goals. Setting an intention is a similar process to setting a goal, but you don't plan out the "how, when and where." The intention is the "why." You just intend the reason you desire the outcome and surrender the process to the Universe. Tracy's story is a living testament to this.

I've been pondering the use of goals and intentions for some time now and I've come to an interesting conclusion. When you are "restless and stuck," it might be a good idea to set goals and plan your way to achieving them. Of course, there's a caveat here: you can't set rigid goals and then punish yourself for not keeping them. You also want to keep your focus *off* what is missing and *on* what it is you desire to accomplish. As you begin to notice more and more success, it becomes easier to live life more spontaneously. Then, you might utilize intentions more fully.

Since this book has been written for those who are just beginning their transformational journey, I've decided to focus on goal-setting initially, but I will also talk about setting intentions and how these are different from goals, so you can find what works best for you.

Goal-Setting

Goal-setting can be a valuable skill. Setting goals can help us focus on things we want to accomplish and move us closer to achieving what we want in life. Goals also serve as a necessary tool to support us in getting out of our stuck patterns. As we grow older, sometimes we have less structure in our lives. This is when it can become even more important to set goals. Goals can keep us motivated, keep us active, and keep us from staying stuck. Having goals to strive for keeps us in the flow of our lives, always moving, thereby avoiding stagnancy. Just be careful to keep checking in with your heart to make sure you are moving in the direction you desire, and notice when your desires change.

If you are anything like me (and I expect you might be), you may have learned about setting business goals at work, or your parents may have taught you about setting financial goals, but you have never been taught about, let alone guided in, how to write personal goal statements to support you in what you want to achieve in life. You are not alone – the vast majority of Goddesses have not been trained, at school or at home, in the importance of documenting personal goals as a tool to support positive, successful life change.

Do you have documented personal goal statements of what you plan to accomplish this week or this month?

 No, Goddesses, a "to do" list of your household chores and planned errands does *not* count as a goal statement!

If not, you probably don't have documented personal statements of what you plan to achieve in the coming five or ten years, or in this lifetime. Let me be clear – I am specifically referring to documented *personal* goals *you* have for *your* life. This is really important, and yet most people don't put a lot of conscious effort into planning for and documenting their life goals.

Think of the last time you went to the grocery store and had to work from a list you had in your head. There you are, trying to rack your brain to come up with all the things you need to buy. I expect you may have forgotten something – perhaps even an important item that was the main thing you went to the store for in the first place, like garbage bags and toilet paper. In your distracted state, you may have even succumbed to some of the in-store specials, sampled offerings of the day, and bought those too. I have done all of this, too!

Now think for a moment on how this experience would have had a better outcome if you had *written* a list of things you needed, first. Now apply this to life goals. The distractions, garbage, and other crap that comes into our life each day can do major damage to our focus on what is really important.

 Oh, and by the way, you can't buy garbage bags or toilet paper for the garbage and s*it that happens in life and even if you could, without your list, you forgot to buy them.

If your goals are not documented or shared, who is holding you accountable for taking action on them? Basically, you're on your own!

This passive approach, the *"I've got my personal goals stored up here"* mentality, often leaves us meandering through life with its inherent distractions. Later, when we look back at our life, many of us regret not having accomplished some of the goals that were once important to us. The problem is further compounded by the fact that most people who hold these goals in their head are simply holding vague goals, not goals that support a structured formula that puts action-taking and success close at hand. Having goals is important, but writing your goals down is the first concrete step in achieving them.

The results of a 2007 research study conducted by Dr. Gail Matthews, a clinical psychologist and tenured professor of psychology at Dominican University in California, can teach us a few lessons on the importance of documenting our goals. With 75% female representation, the study established categorically that writing down our goals *positively increases* the likelihood of achieving those goals. This study also found further positive effects with those individuals who committed to those goals by sharing them with a friend. And finally, there was a positive correlation for those who reported on their goal progress, revealing that accountability also made a significant difference.[57]

So find yourself a supportive, positive-natured friend or family member you can work with on this goal-setting project and give them the authority to be your accountability partner to support your goal achievement.

Personal Goals: Uniquely Our Own

Goal-setting is necessary in supporting us to make improvements and move forward in all areas of our lives. We are all very different people, living in different circumstances, so our goals are uniquely our own. One person's goal could be to find a new job they really enjoy, while another person may have a goal of taking a night school course in cake decorating. Your goal might be to climb a mountain, or write your autobiography. In all cases, a plan documented with the various steps necessary to achieve the goal will go a long way to support it in coming to fruition.

A personal goal is one that will advance *you* in some way; something within you will change. Your level of awareness, growth, or something else in your life will expand as a result of attaining your goal. At times, what happens on the way to achieving a goal is even more important than the final accomplishment itself.

Goals can be internally focused – for example, allocating more of your day to personal time, improving your health and fitness level, letting go of a situation over which you have no control and which is hindering your positive transformation, or letting go of a substance abuse habit.

Goals can also be externally focused, such as visiting a place on your bucket list; or they could include things you would like to

---

[57] http://www.dominican.edu/dominicannews/study-highlights-strategies-for-achieving-goals

acquire, such as a new car, or an oceanfront condo in a warm sunny climate for your retirement.

6 Benefits of Setting and Documenting Personal Goals

As you will note by reviewing this list, there are a host of benefits in setting and documenting your personal life goals. This list is not exhaustive; these are simply six benefits I feel will resonate positively with you.

1. Increases the chances of the journey being a success, just like using a road map or GPS.
2. Highlights our strengths and provides us with personal growth opportunities, thereby positively feeding our self-esteem and self-confidence.
3. Forces us to set priorities, resulting in better time management.
4. Serves as a decision-making guide, e.g. "Does this new planned action support or distract me from my planned goals?"
5. Supports us with a structured framework in various areas of our life, such as health, relationships, lifestyle, and finances.
6. Dissolves doubts. When you start accomplishing various smaller goals to support the bigger goal, you will feel more confident you are on the right path and feel energized to carry on.

It is important to emphasize that personal goals do not have to result in major accomplishments; so if *big* is the only thing that resonates in your mind when you think of the word *goal,* feel free to update your interpretation. Anything you would like to achieve, regardless of size, which supports your personal success or desires in life, qualifies here. All levels of personal goal-setting are important to our future.

So my message to you here is: just get started – set some goals that will help bring you clarity, and focus on the steps necessary to achieve your desires. Another important caveat here, however: we need to ensure we are working toward our *own* goals and desires, not those others have imprinted in our minds.

Work through the exercises in this chapter with the planned outcome of picking a new trajectory for your life (one you absolutely love), and start setting goals to support the optimal life you desire and deserve. Yes, some training and discipline will be required; but once you start to take action on some of the smaller goals that support the larger ones, you will be so pleased with your efforts and the personal growth you have already experienced that you will feel encouraged to do whatever necessary to move further forward.

 I heard a saying once that really resonated with me – goals without action are simply dreams!

In my mind, having a positive attitude is a key component to goal achievement. It keeps you motivated and energized to attain your goals with enthusiasm and confidence. When obstacles get in your way, your positive attitude will go a long way in proactively responding to and moving past these challenges. This is the reason we write our goals with a positive flair.

Beginning With the End in Mind

Stephen Covey, in his book *7 Habits of Highly Successful People,* reminds us to *"begin with the end in mind."* This means you need to determine what you ultimately want to accomplish by the end of this very precious life – what is/are your desired outcome(s)? You then build backwards to design goals that support the outcomes, and further break those objectives into bite-size pieces to support the objectives and ultimately the outcome(s).

If this bigger picture is too much for you to process right now, pick a shorter timeframe that is more comfortable for you. What would you like your life to look like by the end of this year, or at the end of three years? Whatever timeframe you choose, you will identify the end vision you would like to see and then detail the goals you would need to accomplish to achieve this vision.

If you started with a shorter timeframe: when you are ready, based on the positive changes you make as a result of your new learning, you can go back and do this exercise again on a larger scale.

The Goal-Setting Process

At the top of the chart below, I have listed four main goal categories, to keep things simple. Below these, I have listed some of the sub categories (SC) that may be classified under each to help you get started. Feel free to add others I have not listed. Some may also fit under more than one column. There is no right or wrong here. It's more important to capture all of your goals than be concerned with what column they fit into.

Health Goals	Relationship Goals	Lifestyle Goals	Finance Goals
Weight	Self	Career/Job	Savings
Exercise	Life Partner	Community	Salary/Income
Eating habits	Friends	Personal growth	Wealth
Physical	Children	Vacations	$$ For things I want
Mental	Grandchildren	Religion	Philanthropy
Spiritual	Parents	Retirement	
Attitude	Other family	Passion/ Creativity	
		Social	

Here is an example from my own goals, to demonstrate.

My end goal for five years from now is to replace my existing income with new income from my job as an entrepreneur in my own home-based business. Therefore, I need to put a number of goals in place to support this.

1. Leave my job.
2. Create new streams of income from my entrepreneurial endeavors that match 60% of my current income. Yes, that's enough!
3. Have two bestselling self-help books published within this five-year timeframe.

In my example, I am highlighting a lifestyle goal (career/job) that is combined with a financial goal (salary/income). I will walk you through goal 3 to support my five-year plan, so you get a picture of how this could work to complete your own. First, I want to state an important point – this sub-goal is a nice match to my core values. Writing this book feeds my passion for creativity and my desire to grow as a person. It also supports my passion for lifelong learning and personal development, as well as my desire to support others in their own transformational journeys.

Now, back to the example – in order to have two bestselling self-help books in the market in five years, I first need to get this book completed. The intermediary goals needed to achieve this are described below.

Goal 1: Have this book completed and sent to the publisher this summer.

Sub-goal: 1.1 Finish the book revisions by May 30th.

Sub-sub goals: 1.1.1 Finish cleaning up all suggested edits.

1.1.2 Complete a review of all copyright questions.

1.1.3 Re-read all content for best placement.

Sub-goal: 1.2 Find and choose a publisher for the completed book.

Sub-sub goals: 1.2.1 Review publishing contract requirements.

1.2.2 Format based on Balboa Press requirements.

1.2.3 Send completed manuscript to publisher by June 30th.

Note: There may be additional action steps for sub-sub goals that break things down further into weekly and perhaps even daily goals. A complex numbering system is not required; you can simply number your major level goals and then use bullet points for the supporting sub-goals and sub-sub-goals. I used this style to give you a visual of the relationship between these goals. Your turn!

 ## Exercise: Starting to Think about Goal-Setting

Document several goals, and then break them down into the sub-goals and sub-sub-goals necessary to achieve them.

If you don't know yet what your goals are, here are some supporting guidelines. Review the results of your completed exercises from chapters 13-16 on core values, creativity, passions and dreams. Pay special attention to the personal passion-vision statement you crafted in your chapter 15 work. A review of these chapters will likely identify some key goals you haven't really considered before, and will support you in percolating some new goal ideas. Write these all down.

 I hope you are recognizing the interconnectivity of the other chapters to support *your Goddess in the making.*

Next, set aside the time and a quiet space to sit and meditate on this initial list of things you would like to change or acquire in your life. Spend some time over the next few days or weeks meditating on this.

Don't let negative thoughts hold you back. Remember, no more "should-ing." It is important to put on your rose-colored spectacles and then put your pen to paper, or your fingers to the keyboard, and envision your ideal life without considering any supposed lack. This includes time, money, experience, education, or any other perceived lack your ego comes up with to sabotage your success. Promise yourself that you will not give up. You can do this, but your persistence and self-discipline is necessary to ensure success.

 Learning the skill of goal-setting can change your life – and by taking action, you will!

 ## Exercise: Goal-Setting

Now that you have made a list of potential goals and meditated on them, use this exercise to go deeper into firming up your list of goals to support your desires in life. Complete the questions and reflection exercises below, as a starting point.

1. Considering the four main goal categories and sub-categories from the list previously outlined in this chapter, list 6-10 of your previous life accomplishments that you are particularly proud of.

    i. _____

    _____

    _____

    ii. _____

    _____

    _____

    iii. _____

    _____

    _____

    iv. _____

    _____

v. _____

_____

_____

vi. _____

_____

_____

vii. _____

_____

_____

viii. _____

_____

_____

ix. _____

_____

_____

x. _____

_____

_____

2. For each of the above, go back and add who (if anyone) supported you in this accomplishment, as well as their role in this accomplishment (financial, emotional support, cheerleader, or something else).

3. Looking at these past accomplishments, what skills, knowledge, and abilities did you use to achieve them? Make a cumulative list here.

_____

_____

_____

_____

_____

_____

4. The final step is to review your responses for question one. This time, place the word "Yes" in the right-hand margin for any that required a concrete set of goals and sub-goals for you to accomplish them. Alternately, write the word "No" in the right margin for any that did not require any planning, meaning you did nothing; the accomplishment just happened. I doubt you will have many "No" responses when your exercise is completed.

The purpose of this exercise is to demonstrate to yourself that you have achieved some wonderful things in the past. You also know a thing or two already about goal–setting – perhaps not in the formal way presented here, but you are not a virgin to it. The other purpose of this exercise is to help you identify the supports / people resources, knowledge, skills, and abilities you have used before and can bring to the table to support your work in this chapter. If none of this resonates with you, or if goal-setting has not worked for you in the past, perhaps you are a person who would rather set intentions than goals. Do whatever works!

A tip from Mike Dooley: "When visioning, always focus on the end result of whatever it is you want. Don't let other images enter your mind about the hows, whys, and wheres of its attainment."

What Is the Difference between Setting Intentions and Setting Goals?

When discussing goals with Deborah Ivanoff, a successful business coach, she indicated that goal-setting does not work the same for everyone. She stated "that many people get clarity by writing their goals out and they miraculously gather speed in manifesting, and that others need to hold these goals lightly, more as intentions, to prevent expectations from getting in the way of the Universe perhaps offering us something better."[58]

---

[58] Deborah Ivanoff, http://thebeingcoach.com/

The distinctions between goals and intentions make a huge difference in the outcome and the experience. When setting a goal, we think somewhat realistically. We analyze our current situation and plan out steps for how to achieve our objective. Setting goals is a very cognitive process based on analyzing, planning, and reasoning. We are in control of the plan and all the steps to get there.

If you find this process of goal-setting a bit cumbersome, you are not alone. You might even find, like Tracy did, that goal-setting limits you to what you can believe possible. Many spiritual teachers today tell us goal-setting can be a hindrance rather than a help, for that very reason. Sometimes the Universe has far more in mind for us than we think we can achieve. We get caught up in thinking of all the "wrong" things we have to "fix" in our lives before we can accomplish our goals; or we put ourselves down for not yet having attained them, which only sets us back further. If this describes you, you might want to focus on setting intentions instead.

Goals vs. Intentions: A Comparison

- You *see* goals as accomplishments you aspire to; you *feel* intentions as states of being.
- Goals are futuristic; intentions are in the present moment.
- Goals are specific; intentions are broader.
- Goals are external achievements; intentions relate to an inner relationship you have with yourself.
- Goals represent a destination; intentions represent the journey.
- Goals help you make a place in the world; intentions help you live an integral life where balance and oneness is evident.

Here is an example to help you understand the distinct differences. One of my goals is to write this book to support other women in their transformation. It is a *specific* and *futuristic* goal that I can *see* accomplished. It is in alignment with my core values and my passions. A sub-goal of writing the book is to complete a particular chapter before the end of the week. Before I set out on the goal of finishing the chapter, I set the intention of being present with my own journey of personal growth and the opportunity to nourish my creativity along the way.

Now, if I finish writing for the week without having finished the chapter, thereby not achieving the *goal* I set, I will not feel disappointed and overwhelmed. Instead, I will feel encouraged by the new learning and growth I have undergone and the creativity I have exercised, thereby fulfilling my *intention*. The drama of being too attached to the goal outcome is removed from the equation, allowing me to be successful in the intention. For me, partnering goals with intentions can provide the richness you are seeking in life, allowing you to embrace the journey (intentions) in the process of reaching the destination (goal).

 ## Exercise: Setting Intentions

As stated earlier, setting an intention requires putting the when, where, and how aside for a while and just intending with all your heart an outcome that will excite and inspire you. You surrender the process to the Universe, just like making a wish when you blow out the candles on a birthday cake.

Try it out with little things first. Think of an upcoming event; it could be something positive or something you are somewhat dreading. What are some of the situations you will face? What exciting, inspiring outcome would you like? Don't worry if you don't know how it could happen. Just think of the best or most exciting outcome.

Intend it, write it down, put it in safe place, and then let it go. Release it to the Universe and don't worry about *how* it will happen. Just know that the process will be successful. Then you can go about your life having fun and not stressing about every step. The Law of

Attraction brings to us that which we give our attention. In fact, some people like to use the three-step process: Intention, Attention, No Tension. First, decide what it is you'd like to see in your life – people, places, things, and especially qualities. Focus more on the *feeling* and experience these things will bring you, rather than on the items themselves. The only attention you give them is good feelings. Then, release any anxiety about how these objectives will come about.

Similar to goal-setting, some of the challenges people face when setting intentions are really knowing what it is they want and letting go of control over the process of reaching the outcome.

What do you really want? We are often confused because we listen to other people's opinions and to our own self-judgment. Sometimes it can be hard to know if we want something because we want it or because someone else said we *should* want it. So how do you know the difference between the two?

There is a simple way to figure out what is your real desire and what is your "I should." What you want and desire is exciting and inspiring. It comes right out of your being. It makes you happy. What you "should" want causes stress, anxiety, and even depression. It comes from a judgment of how things *should* be, rather than your creative self. So if you are setting an intention or a goal, stop and really listen to your emotions. Your feelings and your heart, not your mind, will always lead you to the perfect result.

Intentions teach us to let go of control. We are so used to thinking we are in control of our lives. We fear the unknown and prefer the status quo. We want to be in control of every step on our way, and this creates a lot of stress if things don't go as planned. Letting go of control is about trusting the Universe will fulfill your intentions.

Try this process more and more, and watch how your trust in the goodness of the Universe grows. You will begin to understand that life is a great adventure, and finally allow the Goddess in you to experience the fun she deserves. Letting go of control creates space in your life where magic happens.

If your personal style is analytical, and you are success-oriented and driven, then by all means, set goals. If the more intuitive approach appeals to you, and you find it easier to set intentions, do that instead – or, as I'm doing, use a bit of both!

You may want to join me in shifting your perspective and creating an empowering relationship between your goals and intentions. I invite you to keep looking for a new way of "seeing" things.

 ## Positive Affirmations Related to Goal-setting and Intentions:

- I am on track to realizing my goals.
- I have crystal-clear goals and/or intentions and desires.
- I take action toward my goals on a daily basis.
- I set a clear intention about every aspect of my life.
- I focus only on what I want and release all anxiety about the *how*.

Chapter 18

Future Adventures – Living Your Authentic Goddess Life with Purpose!

"I work really hard at trying to see the big picture and not getting stuck in ego. I believe we're all put on this planet for a purpose, and we all have a different purpose … When you connect with that love and that compassion, that's when everything unfolds."
Ellen DeGeneres

Goddess Tenet #12: A Goddess strives to be a cheerleader for the common good of all others who exist in this Universe with her.

Goddess Paula, age 56 from Ontario, Canada tells her story:
I needed to press the reset button.
I wanted to bring peace and happiness back into my life and feel like I was doing what I was meant to do.

I was the coordinator and the only full-time professor in my program for six-and-a-half years, and finally we were able to hire another faculty member. Linda was a lovely kind-hearted soul and we worked well together. She had never taught before and I was her mentor, so we spent a lot of time with each other. I finally had someone to bounce program changes off of, and she had a seasoned mentor to support her.

Her first year was eventful. Along with this challenging career change, she got married and enjoyed a trip to Europe for her honeymoon. We both had our holidays that summer, and then September rolled around, bringing the beginning of another school year where we would welcome our students.

On the first day of school, I received a call from her husband. He said she had been in the hospital all weekend and would not be in for the next few days, while they ran some tests. He did not provide further details; he simply stated Linda would call me.

The next day, I got a call that both shocked and devastated me. Linda had been diagnosed with terminal cancer and had just a few short months to live. No warning – she had not even been sick.

I went to visit her in the hospital that weekend and took my husband; I was afraid to go alone. This hospital visit set the tone for the next seven weeks, and so began a series of lessons that strengthened my spirituality and helped me make a number of changes in my life.

Linda and her husband calmly described her funeral, including the food and drinks that would be served following the service. My husband and I both left, shaking our heads in disbelief at the situation. They had accepted her fate and seemed resigned to working pragmatically through what needed to be dealt with. I had thought I would be an emotional mess after the visit and unable to drive, but their calmness and acceptance was infectious.

Linda went home on palliative care within one week of being admitted to the hospital. She invited me to come by weekly and bring her news of our students' progress, and allowed me to share with them continuing news on her situation.

Prior to Linda getting sick, she and I had discussed service learning project ideas for the students, but had not made a final decision as to what this would look like. I had some ideas and, after discussing options in class, the students chose to create a Cookbook for Cancer. It was comprised of a combination of our favorite recipes, and we dedicated the book to Linda. We sold 500 of these at $10 each and donated the $5,000 raised to the local hospital's palliative care unit in her name. Linda knew of this project and chose which recipes she wanted to submit. I gave her an update of the project's status at each of my weekly visits.

During these visits, not once in the seven short weeks did I ever see her shed one tear, nor did she ever say, *"Why me?"* We sat and talked each week, like she was recovering from an operation. Two of the life-changing lessons she taught me were how to accept with grace a situation over which we have no control and what it is to be extremely brave while facing death. There were so many more.

Before I even knew of her illness, I had another service learning project I had been trying to get administrative support for at the college. The project was called the Pink Glove Dance. The Pink Glove Dance is an amazing opportunity for whole organizations to work together to raise awareness for breast cancer research. This project would inspire our community to work together toward a common goal and have a lot of fun doing it.

I started each of my classes with an inspirational video. For one class I chose the Pink Glove Dance. It demonstrated the requirement of a lot of planning to bring a project to completion. As this was a project-planning class, this was a good choice. Linda knew of this project; we had discussed it a number of times. After several of my weekly visits, I hesitantly approached her with my idea to include her in it by dubbing her video clip into the final video, pending the college's approval to go ahead with the project. Unbelievably, she said yes!

In the Pink Glove Dance, everyone puts on pink clothing and accessories and shakes their booty in some way, to music. I gave Linda a pink t-shirt and the very next week when I arrived, I knew she was still on track, as she was wearing it.

Linda only had two outings in the seven weeks she spent at home on palliative care: one for blood work and one to go to Walmart with her husband to buy a ladies' extra-large turtleneck for him and two pairs of pink pajama pants, a pair for each of them.

The day I was to go to their home after class to record them dancing, I went out to buy the pink gloves. I drove all over town and went to four separate stores to find two pairs in two suitable sizes for each of them, before driving to their home. With less than three weeks until her passing, this very brave woman danced with her husband to the Pink Glove Dance song while I videotaped the few precious moments in time.

To top off this whole amazing story, in the last week of her life, she gave me a thank you card. In the card, she thanked me for my compassion and stated she wished she had known me for a greater portion of her life. She also encouraged me to go after my higher purpose, stating that I had so much more to give to humanity.

That message went a long way in my decision a year later to leave my job. This was not an easy decision, but I knew there were new things in store for me where I could use the skills, knowledge, and abilities I had gained in my life, and I was anxious to explore them. I was ready for the challenge of a new adventure. I had an important mission – to pursue my life's purpose! I already knew of this entrepreneurial tug that was pulling on my heartstrings.

My passionate desire was and still is to use my knowledge, skills, and attributes to inspire, mentor, and empower women to transform their own lives through personal development, with the ultimate goal of pursuing their goals, dreams, and life purpose!

I learned that Linda had successfully battled ovarian cancer several decades before and had undergone all the usual rigorous cancer treatments. She had also lost a son, Ben, when he was only 19 years old. I now recognized she knew far before the rest of us that this was her destiny. She told me at one point she was going home to be with Ben again.

From Linda, I learned about bravery in the face of death and the tenacity of one woman's spirit. I learned about love, and that one person's wisdom can change another's life forever. Thank you, Linda, for being my friend – and thank you for imparting those final words of *wisdom that went a long way in encouraging me to pursue an adventure in living true to my life's purpose.*

All readers of this book are likely sending you private whispers of thanks too, because of the ripple effect your message inspired.

* * *

Life is not meant to be something we simply get through. It is designed to be so much more. Life is full of adventures, and it is from those adventures that we learn important lessons. We will make mistakes in life. That's often how we learn, and it's why we're here!

Personally, I have been told by a number of Intuitives and Psychics that I have lived many lifetimes. I have been told I was born an old soul and that my mission is to learn new life lessons, lessons I did not master in previous lives.

 Apparently, I must have fallen asleep in class in the past!

I am a conscious and willing student of life and I am ready, willing, and able to pay attention this time around and participate in this amazing adventure in learning.

 Congratulations, Goddess! I expect you are ready, too, as you have reached the last chapter of this book!

Challenge Yourself with a New Adventure!

Attending the Mike Dooley Infinite Possibilities Train the Trainer program proved to be quite an adventure. I flew five-and-a-half hours from Toronto to Los Angeles, where I took an hour-long bus ride to Ventura Beach. I was going to a place I had never been, where I didn't know a soul. I would spend a lot of money and close to a week by myself in various hotels in a different country, based on blind faith after watching a short video that convinced me this training program was exactly what I needed at this point in my life. I liken how I felt to "love at first sight."

That little bit of anxiety I felt, common to any new adventure, was instantly washed away when, at the end of the bus ride, I met another woman attending the same training. She was part of the planning team and immediately took me under her wing. She invited me to lunch, where I was introduced to a core group of other "trailblazer" trainers, meaning they had trained at least eight other people for a minimum eight hours each.

Sometimes we think about doing something and we want to do it, but we put it off for one reason or another. I want to remind you, though, there is no such day as someday; and I caution you not to let *"one* of these days" turn into *"none* of these days."

Even though I am an introvert, I challenged myself with a new adventure and it paid off ten-fold. Isn't it time *you* took part in a little adventure?

 And when I say adventure, I don't mean bungee jumping off the Kawarau Bridge in New Zealand – a new learning adventure will suffice!

Expand Your Circle of Love

I found the adventure of attending this training to be an invaluable experience in my journey to living my life purpose. In addition, I greatly expanded my circle of love. The Infinite Possibilities community is comprised of like-minded people who spread a message of hope. They truly care, support, and give of themselves – characteristics aligned with my own beliefs and philosophy!

Through this experience, I found my "tribe." Even when the conference ended, I could tell these new friends would be lasting connections because of the powerful bond we shared. This training came at a perfect time, as I was just finishing the first draft of this, the 18th and final chapter. The new things I learned complemented all I had been writing about and would certainly influence my second draft review.

For me, life is a transformational journey. We are on a personal quest for greater meaning and purpose in our existence. Believing in and spreading the news that life is a gift, a joyful experience, and a wonderful adventure of learning will go a long way in enhancing and expediting our journey. This will not only benefit us as individual Goddesses, but the Universe in its entirety.

 Positive Paula at her finest!

Whenever you *see* something you could use more of – let's use love as an example – start by *being* more love and *giving* more love. You'll be amazed at the way your outer world (the love you get back) begins to reflect your inner dimension (the love you desire).

I invite you to consider expanding your circle of love by finding places where you can connect with like-minded people who have similar goals and beliefs. They help you grow! This experience may well be the ticket to living your own life with purpose.

Positive Affirmations Related to Adventuring and Living Life with Purpose:

- I do not need anyone's permission to be my true self.
- I say YES to the messages from my heart and soul.
- I release the familiar so that I may better discover my inspiring future.
- Life is a fun and pleasurable adventure. I play with life, laugh with life, dance with life, and smile at the riddles of life.

Conclusion

Life represents a series of small miracles. It is a constant adventure, filled with delight. When we find ourselves stuck, we are not allowing the richness and beauty that surrounds us into our lives. I am grateful every day that I managed to get unstuck, that I found this path, and that I have the joy of sharing it with other women. I have found my passion and live my life with purpose. All of this **is** available for **you**, too.

Begin where you are, right now. Read and re-read these chapters until you breathe these ideas. The concepts I have shared are universal practices, and their staying power is testament to one thing – they work! If you yearn to create the life you truly want to live, you need to incorporate these principles into your daily life. Your new reality includes seeing yourself and your life from a new perspective. You now have the tools to unthaw, to shift from where you were to becoming the Goddess you are meant to be – that self-compassionate being who supports you, nourishes you, and loves you.

 After all, I hope you have realized by this point, that it is **all about you!**

The world has shifted so tremendously since my childhood that it sometimes overwhelms me when I look at all the potential we have today. No one else is responsible for our being and becoming whatever we desire. It is remarkable to think that a simple shift in how we think is enough to trigger an opening in consciousness and alter our perceptions of our lives entirely. And that shift in how we think is possible for any of us, if we choose to make it.

I knew I had a purpose and a desire to empower women and help them flourish into their true essence – and here I am. I have now written a book, and am blessed to have you read it. I have my own business and my own brand. I am living my dreams and enjoying my life more now than ever. And this rebirth of sorts happened in my mid-50s.

As women, we are blessed with powerful bodies that constantly remind us of our own evolution. Instead of denying the aging process, I am diving headfirst into it. Instead of fighting my body's changing hormones, I celebrate the new stage of womanhood I am entering. I encourage all of you to do the same. Celebrate your femininity, at any stage of life. Celebrate the wisdom of aging …

 … and being someone who knows shit!

We are a vital tribe of wise Goddesses – and the most powerful years are yet to come. It's never too late to take action, to find and give to yourself the way you have been giving to so many throughout your life. It is never selfish to love yourself. It is never too late to try something new, like taking a salsa dance class or learning to play the piano. To paraphrase the famous quote by Mary Oliver, *"We have one wild, precious life. Tell me, how do you plan to spend yours?"*

I hope this book has inspired you to be open to experiencing every opportunity that will help you grow, learn, love, and transform. I trust you have realized that understanding who you *are* and who you are *becoming* is paramount to embracing transformation. Become an example to others of someone who has adjusted her attitude and is living true to herself with self-love as her highest priority; someone who has chosen joy and authenticity as her mantra; someone who is living her Goddess life with purpose. It's time to live your life full out and unencumbered by your past. It's time to take better care of yourself and focus on the positive. Surrender to the beauty of your true self – learn to play again, dance again, love again, and learn again.

Brilliant physicist Albert Einstein once said, "There are two ways to live life: one is as though nothing is a miracle; the other" – and my hands-down favorite option – "is to live life as though everything is." Keep looking for a new way of *seeing* things and you will experience a new way of *being*. I invite you to go forth with this philosophy; and while you're at it, remember you are not here merely to survive – you are truly meant to thrive.

Now What?

Live Bold and Shine Brightly, Goddess!
Ongoing support and community are critical for success in any area of your life. One of the biggest factors in my own ongoing growth and overall wellness has been the group of Goddesses holding one another accountable, being guides for each other, cheering one another on, supporting and loving one another. I want this for you, too.

This book is only the beginning of your love affair with yourself. There is a whole lot more fun ahead.

Below, I've put together more resources, education, programs, tools, and ongoing Goddess social support opportunities for you.

a. Website: Sign up for future Goddess community mailings at www.transformingvenus.com. Access exclusive webinars, videos, programs, recommendations, interviews, and articles. The material in this book is living and breathing in my own life. As I find and create new material, I'll be sure to share it with you on the site. As a thank you gift, when you sign up, you'll receive my free seven-week audio adventure, *Letting Your Inner Goddess out to Play*.

b. Facebook: By liking the page, you will receive the Goddess Gems and be part of the Facebook Goddess community. ww.facebook.com/TransformingVenus

c. Twitter: Follow us on Twitter using #TransformVenus.

And finally, I'd love to hear from you and how this material has enhanced your life. Please share your stories at success@ transformingvenus.com

Notes

Printed in the United States
By Bookmasters